D0745249

BROADVIEW LIBRAR

garden design

REFRESH YOUR GARDEN DESIGN WITH COLOR, TEXTURE & FORM

NO LONGER PROPERTY OF
SEATTLE PUBLIC LIBRARY

REFRESH YOUR
GARDEN DESIGN
WITH COLOR, TEXTURE & FORM

REBECCA SWEET

Horticulture

CINCINNATI, OHIO
WWW.GARDENERSHUB.COM

DEDICATION:

This book is dedicated to my mother, Linda Anderson, who led me down this garden path many years ago.

ACKNOWLEDGMENTS:

This book has been simmering in my mind for many years, slowly revealing itself in the gardens I've designed for others, in the garden I've created for myself, and in my writing. However, it's taken the proverbial horticultural village—in the form of the many friends I've made through the Association of Professional Landscape Designers, blogging, and social media—to bring this idea to fruition. Thank you all for your insightful expertise, passion, and encouragement! And to my inspiring clients: I am forever indebted to you for bravely allowing me to join you in the creation of your gardens. Your trust in me has been invaluable.

I especially wish to acknowledge a few people dear to my heart, for their generosity in opening their unforgettable gardens to me and my trusty camera: Jon and Linda Anderson, Lisa Mitchell, and Freeland and Sabrina Tanner. And to my amazing husband, Tom, and daughter, Emily: Where would I be without you? Thank you for once again coming along on this thrilling ride with me.

To my editorial cohorts: Patty Craft, Christine Doyle and Christy Cotterman—thank you for your patience and amazing skills in knowing just the right thing to say, how to wield the mighty red pen, and the ability to turn a conceptual dream into a reality.

CONTENTS

INTRODUCTION

What is it about certain gardens that cause our hearts to beat a little faster while slowing our pace and causing us instinctively to reach for our cameras? And how do these gardens end up lodged in our memories for years to come? We've seen plenty of other beautiful gardens, but what makes these particular gardens take our breath away?

The answer is simple: harmony. While strolling through one of these magical gardens, no matter its style, you sense that all the elements seem to click, resulting in an unexpected and delightful experience, far away from the outside world. If you were to dissect one of these gardens, you'd notice it consists of several timeless building blocks of design (such as color, texture, line and form) that are layered in such a way that, when viewed as a whole, creates this stunning effect.

However, the ability to identify harmony in a garden is one thing, while creating it is another. Out of the hundreds of new clients I've met with over the years, the most common complaint I've heard is their overall dissatisfaction with the lack of harmony in their gardens. They may have been happy with their gardens at one time, but somewhere along the line things changed.

Don't worry; it happens to everyone at some point. One day you stroll out to your garden, steaming cup of coffee in hand, and the realization hits you like a ton of bricks: This is *not* the garden I had in mind when I created it! While you may have had good intentions at the time, something happened to your garden over the years, causing it to look unorganized, disheveled and mismatched. Like it's weary and just rolled out of bed.

Your garden isn't what it once was, and you don't know why. This realization results in frustration at not knowing when, where or how to refresh your garden's design in an effort to restore harmony to your garden. A sinking feeling sets in as you assume the only solution is to rip everything out and start from scratch. To say you're feeling overwhelmed is an understatement.

If you find yourself nodding your head in agreement, then you're reading the right book. *Refresh Your Garden Design With Color, Texture & Form* overflows with photos and illustrations that will both inspire and inform. I'm also happy to tell you that garden transformations don't necessarily require an expensive overhaul by a team of professionals. Sometimes all it takes is a fresh perspective, and a new way to look at your garden. In chapter one, *Seeing With Fresh Eyes*, you'll

The contrasting colors of the two sweet potato vines (*Ipomoea spp.*) create a dynamic yet simple focal point.

learn tips and techniques to help you become your own garden designer. Learn how to look at your garden with fresh eyes, not only to pinpoint specific problem areas but to identify solutions to fix them.

In many ways chapter two, *Color*, is the heart of this book, as more often than not, color is at the root of a garden's harmony (or lack thereof). You'll not only learn about the transformative powers of color but how to use them to refresh your garden in unconventional and creative ways.

Harmony, however, is multidimensional, consisting of many different layers that work together. In chapter three, *Texture*, you'll learn how to add this layer to your garden in ways you may not have thought of before. More than just an afterthought, texture is a key element that adds necessary dimension in a garden.

Remember geometry? In chapter four, *Form*, you'll discover the difference between shape and form and how to use these two powerful concepts in the garden. Learn to create optical illusions, change a garden's mood and carry your garden through the year.

The final chapter in this book, chapter five, *Plant Picks*, is a thoughtfully curated selection of plants, each chosen to help you create a specific element of harmony in your garden: color, texture, shape and form.

Within each chapter you'll discover Design Spotlights that deconstruct a garden vignette to help further illustrate a specific design concept.

So despair no more! Once you understand how your garden's different layers work together, it will be fun (and easy!) to refresh your garden's design. Get ready to transform it into the garden you have always dreamed about.

CHAPTER 1

SEEING WITH FRESH EYES

A lush planting mix emphasizing color, texture and form breathes new life into my own garden, which is more than forty years old.

As a designer, I know firsthand that creating a garden from scratch is infinitely easier than designing around an established garden, one that's already filled in with existing plants and hardscaping. Decisions such as which plants to keep, which to toss, how to incorporate new colors or how to add year-round interest are just a sampling of those that need to be addressed. Learning to see your garden through fresh eyes is often the first step in helping refresh your garden.

WHERE TO BEGIN

As you stand there looking at your lackluster garden with decisions and questions filling your head, it becomes increasingly apparent that you may not know quite where to begin. Not sure exactly what it is you don't like about your garden, you begin to ask yourself a million questions: Should I try to save these plants over here? Can I add a few more shrubs to help fill out that area? What about introducing an arbor? It's no wonder home gardeners throw their hands up in frustration and go back inside for the rest of the day!

Before you're able to implement solutions to refresh your garden though, you first need to identify the problems it currently has.

To do this effectively, it's important to understand *how* to look at your garden with fresh eyes. This concept may seem straightforward enough, but it's often difficult to accomplish.

Something we designers refer to as "familiarity blindness" can develop over the years, making it increasingly difficult for clients to objectively look at their gardens. When the gardener and the garden have been having the same conversation every day for years, it becomes challenging to see things in a new light. It seems the longer a person lives with a garden, the worse this blindness actually is!

Sometimes it's easy to determine what you don't like about your garden (for example, dead plants that need to be replaced or an obvious eyesore that needs to be hidden), though it's usually not that simple. More often than not, the garden is in fairly decent shape with no glaring issues, making it all the more difficult to identify areas that could use some improving.

So where and how do you begin?

DESIGN TIP

When thinking of ways to breathe life back into your garden, gather together articles from magazines or newspapers and inspirational garden photos. Spread them out on a table and group them into categories of similarities. You'll begin to see consistencies emerge, such as what your favorite colors are, or the style of garden that you gravitate toward (contemporary vs. cottage, for example), or even the plants you lean toward (spiky or bold vs. soft or wispy). These are all clues that can help you figure out where to begin your garden's transformation.

It's easy to breathe new life back into your garden once you learn how to look at it with fresh eyes.

Top: An artful mix of color, texture and form, combined with a cool color palette, results in an intriguing and restful garden bed.

Bottom: Carefully selected garden art, such as this antique birdbath, provides a garden with personality and unique charm.

EDIT TO ENHANCE

While it might sound overly simple, an important step to seeing your garden with fresh eyes is to remove the clutter. Unless a gardener has an unusual amount of self-control, most gardens have accumulated their fair share of ornaments, decorations, mementos and kitsch. You know, the items we couldn't pass up at the quaint garden shop? Or the garden-related *art* our friends and family have given us at each and every holiday?

As part of my design process, I take plenty of before, during and after photos of a client's garden. Time and time again, my clients are rendered speechless while looking at the before photos, shocked at how their garden resembles a giant garage sale—a result of familiarity blindness, to be sure.

Without passing judgment on a person's taste in garden décor, remember this rule of thumb: Garden art should *enhance* your garden, not distract from it. I'm not suggesting permanently removing all of these items from your garden, but instead, temporarily setting them aside. The purpose of this first step is to make it easier to focus on the plants themselves in an effort to help diagnose problem areas.

DESIGN TIP

Mementos are always a delightful touch in the garden, adding charm and personality. An easy way to begin adding these personal touches to your garden is to collect items from nature, such as shells, driftwood or seedpods. These natural materials will seamlessly blend in with your garden. Too many small items scattered around the garden, however, can quickly create a cluttered effect. To prevent this from happening, group like items together in one area, resulting in both a stronger impact as well as a tidier look.

Children's art is at home in any garden, and when carefully placed, it is a heartwarming reminder of bygone times.

EDIT AND SHRED IT

"Edit, edit and edit again" is a common mantra garden designers use to help reinforce the importance of exercising restraint in the garden. When seeing a blank space in a garden bed, it's human nature to want to rush out and fill it with the latest and greatest find at the nursery. While planting every square inch of a garden may be an effective technique to quickly achieve lush and full results, it can easily backfire. An overplanted garden not only results in a cluttered looking, less-than-harmonious space, it also quietly harbors a whole host of potential problem areas. An overgrown garden also makes it difficult to spot the plants that are ailing or outright dead.

This is the time to take a good, long look at your garden to identify and remove those poorly performing plants and introduce them to your composter. Everyone seems to have a few of these plants lurking in his or her garden; plants that are nursed along year after year, limping along at best and never living up to their full potential. If you feel guilty about ripping them out, remember the wise words of renowned horticulturist J.C. Raulston: "If you're not killing plants, you're not really stretching yourself as a gardener." So consider the removal of dead and dying plants a version of personal gardening growth—it's a necessary step in your garden's evolution.

By removing these intruders on your garden's design, you've further decluttered your garden, making it much easier to determine what the next steps should be.

Unfortunately, the half dead rosemary, ailing grasses and past-their-prime thyme are taking center stage in this weary garden bed.

DESIGN TIP

One way to turn garden garbage into garden gold is to compost your dead and dying plants. If your plants are diseased, however, take care when composting and consider throwing the plants in the garbage instead to avoid future contamination.

EDIT YOUR EXPECTATIONS

When writing a book, one of the benefits of working with an editor is their ability to point out when you may have veered down the wrong road. Even though you are creating a garden rather than a book it's important that you act as your garden's editor to help reassess the road you're on and determine whether or not you need to switch gears.

Take a step back and look at your garden with a critical eye to see if the result before you matches your original intent. For example, your original goal might have been to create a sleek and contemporary garden that would blend seamlessly with your home's geometric lines. However, what you see before you is an overplanted garden filled with exuberant, free-flowing plants, spilling this way and that, with only a tad bit of structure scattered here and there.

Study your garden's overall design, and you might very well see a combination of one, two or even three styles resulting in a visually jarring space. Perhaps it's time to acknowledge that your tastes may have changed over the years. There's a certain amount of freedom that comes from a realization such as this. No longer bound by the expectations of having your garden fit within a certain style means you're free to embrace what you've been yearning for and run with it!

DESIGN TIP

One way to avoid a clash between two styles that seem entirely unrelated is to use *transitional plants* throughout the garden. Transitional plants are those that are at home in both styles, and when used throughout the entire garden, they can help knit the two styles together.

The structural forms of juncus are subtly echoed by the casual forms of the ornamental grasses, helping blend this garden's modern and casual aesthetics.

Shutterstock.com / Dragos

A photo eliminates distractions, such as cars whizzing by, bike riders and chatty neighbors, allowing you to take a leisurely approach to studying your garden's needs.

YOUR CAMERA:
YOUR PERSONAL GARDEN DESIGNER

After you've decluttered your garden, one of the most effective tools to help see it with fresh eyes is one you probably already own: a camera. As I mentioned earlier, one of the things I do when visiting a client's garden for the first time is to take lots of photos. I not only take photos before we begin the project, but during and after, as well. I refer to these photographs constantly during the design process, as they not only remind me of the garden while I'm physically away from it, but they also allow me to keep a record of the garden's progress over a long period of time.

But more importantly, looking at a garden while *away* from the garden eliminates all distractions. Gone are the chirping birds, the burbling fountain, the planes flying overhead or the neighbor's barking dog. Without these distractions, the focus is entirely on the garden itself. This is a highly effective, and remarkably easy, way to take a more objective look at your garden.

Knowing how and when to use your camera in your garden is like having your own personal garden designer at your beck and call. The first step is easy: take plenty of photos, both close-up and a little farther away, of your garden bed's problematic areas. If your garden bed needs help with more than one or two distinct areas, take a few steps back to capture as much of the garden bed as you can within one or two frames.

The next step is to print out the photos. Make yourself comfortable in a quiet spot in your home and study them. Like an optical illusion, when you look at the photos long enough, you'll begin to notice all sorts of new things about your garden that you never noticed before.

CLASHING COLORS

As you begin studying your photographs, one of the first things you'll notice is a heightened awareness of color. While you may have thought combining pink and orange was a perfectly good idea at the time, the photograph might point out this combination's jarring effect. Making pink and orange work together depends on other factors as well, such as subtle shades and hues, other nearby colors and surrounding foliage.

On the other hand, you may have thought you were creating a green and serene garden consisting of soothing shades of green, gray and white. However, what you see before you in the photograph is a garden that's somewhat monotonous and downright boring, with no real distinction from one plant to the next (more about using color in chapter two).

FILL IN THE BLANKS

While looking at these photos, you may also become acutely aware of areas of your garden bed that now have empty holes where thriving plants once lived. It's one thing to overplant a garden and another to have one that's inconsistently threadbare.

As you wonder why you never noticed that blank spot before, keep in mind this is a common result of familiarity blindness. As you've been walking around your garden, your mind has been subconsciously registering that blank space as having been the former home of the original plant. Photos tend to show the obvious, so you now realize there's a gaping hole just waiting for its new inhabitant.

While there's plenty of color contrast in this vignette, perhaps the smoldering red and cool blue colors are too drastically different for this restful garden.

An all-green garden can be lush and relaxing; however, the missing contrast of shades, texture and form can result in a lackluster combination.

EYESORES GALORE

It seems all gardens, despite their size, have something in them that the homeowner finds less than desirable. These eyesores might be necessary parts of life (such as garbage areas or air conditioning units), but this doesn't mean we have to look at them from every angle of the garden. There is a multitude of gardening techniques that discreetly divert attention from the eyesore. Unfortunately, the longer someone lives with a garden, the more likely the offending eyesore will become one of the first casualties of familiarity blindness.

When walking in your garden, it's natural to glance quickly over the unsightly composter lurking in the corner, preferring instead to focus on a more attractive area. However, when looking at your garden in a photograph, it's not quite as easy to visually skip over these objects. The photograph's honesty forces you to acknowledge their existence. Perhaps it's an unsightly downspout, bulky utility box or the neighbor's basketball hoop looming over the fence. No matter what you call it, it's an eyesore, and it needs to be addressed.

A combination of plants and artwork helps draw the eye's attention away from the neighbor's greenhouse roof.

While you may not be able to entirely eliminate an eyesore from your garden, you can certainly reduce its visual impact with creative plant placement.

DESIGN TIP

Air conditioning units are often placed in less-than-desirable locations in the garden. However, use caution when covering up this particular eyesore, as you don't want to block the unit's air circulation, resulting in a malfunctioning machine. Another concern is the hot air blown out by these units, potentially burning nearby plants. Space the plants one to two feet from the unit to provide necessary screening without causing damage to the unit. Don't forget to leave one side of the A/C unit open and unplanted for periodic maintenance.

DESIGN SPOTLIGHT

DREARY TO DAZZLING

Before The impressive flax (*Phormium tenax* 'Atropurpureum'), with its deep chocolate colors and striking form, is clearly the star of this garden bed. All divas, however, need a supporting cast to help them shine and put their best foot forward. Unfortunately, the lack of form, foliage and color contrasts surrounding this flax all divert attention away from the star performer and onto the uninspired ensemble.

After Placing the container within the garden bed not only helps counterbalance the dark and heavy colors of the flax and loropetalum, it provides additional height and interest, as well.

BEFORE

AFTER

1. The curling, twisting branches of the Harry Lauder's walking stick (*Corylus avellana* 'Contorta') provide form and winter interest.

2. The cool blue foliage of the spurge (*Euphorbia characias* ssp. *wulfenii*) and nearby hens-and-chicks succulents (*Echeveria* 'Imbricata') provide a welcome change of color.

3. The gold and amber foliage colors from the evergreen silverberry (*Elaeagnus* × *ebbingei* 'Gilt Edge') and the nearby mirror plant (*Coprosma repens* 'Tequila Sunrise') visually pops against the surrounding sea of green.

4. The loose, billowy forms of the dwarf mat rush (*Lomandra longifolia* 'Breeze'), pictured, and Berkeley sedge (*Carex divulsa*) provide motion (when blown by a breeze) as well as contrasting form and foliage shapes.

CONNECT THE DOTS

Oftentimes a garden bed is just about perfect the first year it's created. Every plant sings in harmony with its neighbor, flowering perennials are strategically placed to provide year-round blooms, and the garden is filled with drifts of color that seamlessly knit one section to the next.

But something happens to these harmonious garden beds over the years, and as you stroll through your garden, what lies before you now is a little bit of this and a little bit of that, with no real rhyme or reason. It's natural to become a little overwhelmed with what you see while standing in your garden, which is all the more reason to use photographs to help pinpoint exactly what went wrong.

In a photograph you can quickly point out any broken forms in your garden bed. For example, a common design strategy is to plant in odd numbers (three, five, seven, etc.). When these odd-numbered plants are placed in a staggered pattern, the seemingly random form created tends to look more natural in the landscape. While there are certainly exceptions to this rule, more often than not, using odd-numbered plants is a good rule of thumb. Problems arise when a few of the plants die over the years, resulting in oddly spaced numbers that have a visually jarring effect.

This is something I see time and again in client gardens. At one point, there may have been a gentle curving drift of seven plants connecting one garden bed to the next. However, over the years, three of the center plants disappeared. Now all that remains are two disjointed and somewhat linear clumps that look oddly out of place.

The smaller and more compact the form, such as a triangle, the more important it is to make sure the shape remains intact. A loosely spaced triangular pattern creates visual depth in a garden. However, if one of the three plants dies, the depth is lost and the two remaining plants create a direct line. This choppy line can often look awkward and out of place. Fortunately, once the broken form is identified, the solution can be as simple as filling the holes left by the missing plants.

Top: The placement of the two blue grasses creates an unnatural line between them.

Bottom: Adding a third grass creates a triangular shape and a more natural line.

Page 23: A drift of blue violas and a few ornamental glass balls (in coordinating colors) further connect the trio of grasses.

DESIGN TIP

When creating a pathway through the garden, it's essential to think about its intended purpose. If it is to be a functional path, one that is wider with a level surface will accommodate transporting a wheelbarrow or garbage bin. A wider path will also make it easier for two people to leisurely stroll side by side throughout the garden. On the other hand, a narrow path can appear more intriguing, quietly beckoning one to travel the road less taken when exploring the garden that lies beyond. Whichever width you choose, to encourage visitors to walk down the path, the entry point needs to be clearly indicated and inviting.

LACK OF FLOW

A garden's lack of flow is never more apparent than in a photograph. You may know very well how to get from one area in your garden to another, however it may not be so obvious to a visitor. Have you ever hosted a garden party where everyone remains firmly planted on the patio, and try as you might, you can't get people to budge? It's frustrating when no one wanders throughout your garden, exploring the masterpiece that you worked so hard to create.

Quite often the answer is a missing or obstructed pathway that results in a garden's lack of flow. Look at your photograph. Is there a pathway wide enough for two people to comfortably stroll side by side? Or is it obstructed and uninviting as a result of overgrown plants? Perhaps the pathway is lacking all together, with nothing more than a few casually placed (and barely visible) stepping-stones. In either case, nothing beats the honesty of a photograph to point out this much-needed area of improvement.

This narrow pathway is unobstructed, level and clearly visible. Combined with the focal point olive jar, it beckons visitors to explore the garden beyond.

The wide brick pathway is not only inviting but wide enough to accommodate useful wheelbarrows and garbage bins.

While this narrow pathway is indeed intriguing, due to the intruding and oversized plants, visitors are likely to feel hesitant to explore the garden.

OUT OF BALANCE

When looking at a photo of your garden bed, does your eye tend to gravitate to one side versus the other? Does the bed look a little lopsided? This is most likely the result of several factors, such as an uneven mix of colors and shades (light vs. dark, for example), drastic size differences or shapes that are out of scale with one another. All of these can be easily remedied with solutions discussed throughout this book.

Having an unbalanced garden bed is one thing, but having an entire garden out of balance is another. For example, when people come to visit, have you noticed they tend to gravitate to one side over another? Look at your garden photographs taken at a distance. Does your eye naturally transition from one side to the other? Or is your attention drawn to one particular area? Perhaps it's a result of spatial differences, with one side having much wider garden beds than the other. Or perhaps it's an optical illusion created by a mismatched combination of plants. Either way, this is one more example of how a photograph can help bring the somewhat elusive concept of balance to your attention.

The visually imposing shrub on the right, coupled with the delicate and airy plants on the left, creates a very lopsided effect.

Even though the majority of the plants are on the left side of this garden, the bold color blue running throughout the pathway helps restore visual balance.

This lush green garden has a pleasing mix of green, burgundy and gold colors.

Once the color is removed, however, a lack of contrast is evident in the shades of the colors as well as the shapes and sizes of the different foliage.

SOMETIMES IT'S AS SIMPLE AS BLACK AND WHITE

Ready to have your new personal garden designer work a little harder for you? While still on your computer, run the digital photos of your garden through a photo-altering computer program (many of which are free) to strip away one of the biggest distractions of all: color. Transforming your color photos to black and white is like taking an X-ray of your garden. These X-rays are powerful tools to help you see your garden in an entirely new light.

Color is such a complex element, made up of several factors such as *hue* (the actual name of the color, such as red), *intensity* (the brightness of a color) and *value* or *shade* (the lightness or darkness of a color). It's no wonder our brains register color first when looking at a garden, and it's what we usually spend the most time admiring. Black-and-white photographs remove the hues and intensities of color, allowing us to focus on a color's less obvious aspects, such as brightness or value. By eliminating the more obvious aspects of color, the subtle (yet important) problem areas in your garden are now easier to identify. Problem areas such as lack of contrast, shapeless forms or lack of winter interest now come into focus, allowing you to look at your garden in a new light.

FADING FOLIAGE

One of the greatest strengths of a black-and-white photograph is that you can clearly identify contrast, or lack thereof. Quite often when looking at a garden bed that's in fairly decent shape, it's difficult to determine what, exactly, needs improving. Even when focusing on just a small section of that bed, distracting elements such as color can mask any obvious flaws. Look at that same vignette in black and white, however, and a problem such as lack of contrast becomes quickly apparent. While there very well may be plenty of contrast in color, you may discover a lack of contrast in texture or form is the culprit of a less-than-exciting combination.

SHAPELESS FORMS

In addition to highlighting contrasting foliage shapes, a black-and-white photograph also helps point out a garden bed's forms. While similar in concept, form and shape are two different things. The concept of shape is commonly applied to a plant's foliage, consisting of two dimensions: height and width. Examples of a leaf's shape include adjectives such as round, pointed or palmate. The concept of form, however, applies to the overall outline of the plant, and consists of three dimensions: height, width and depth. Examples of a plant's form might include weeping, conical or spherical.

As mentioned, when looking at a color photograph of a garden, the eye tends to focus on color first, making it difficult to determine what areas need improving. Look at that same photo with the color removed and it becomes apparent whether or not the individual plants have enough distinctive form separating them from one another to make an impact. Study the black-and-white photo to see if there's more than one form in the garden bed. If your photo consists primarily of only one or two forms, this area may need your attention.

A restful combination of hakone grass (Hakonechloa macra 'Aureola') and Japanese forest grass needs something to help it stand out from the crowd.

Once the color is removed, the plants seem to morph into one another, demonstrating a total lack of contrast in shading, shape and form.

WINTER'S WASTELAND

With or without a photograph, there's no escaping a garden's lack of form when viewing it in the midst of winter's grip. If your garden consists mainly of perennials and annuals, with the occasional shrub or tree, then you're undoubtedly aware of the immense flatness of it all once winter arrives.

If you happen to garden in a snowy climate, it's even more apparent whether or not your garden contains creative combinations of form and structure. Similar to a black-and-white photograph, a snow-kissed garden has removed the distraction of color. Why not combine the power of winter with the power of a black-and-white photo to take the ultimate X-ray of your garden to unlock its hidden potential?

Take advantage of winter's quiet months and thoroughly study those photographs, playing around with the idea of introducing different forms. One way to help you envision how your garden might look is to cut different forms from paper and move them around on your photograph. Interesting forms to try might include vertical shrubs (such as *Ilex crenata* 'Sky Pencil'), spherical shrubs (such as *Pittosporum tenuifolium* 'Golf Ball') or weeping forms (such as *Morus alba* 'Pendula'). Never will it be more obvious where to introduce a strong form than now!

Once the roses are dormant and pruned, the lack of year-round form in this perennial garden bed becomes evident, resulting in a less-than-exciting winter garden.

A light dusting of snow beautifully highlights the strong forms of the espaliered arbor, rounded shrubs and garden art.

Striking when viewed up close, the finely cut foliage and wispy blooms of the curry plant (*Helichrysum italicum*) are echoed by the lavender in the distance.

When viewed from afar, the silvery foliage and mass of blooms remain a presence when planted in drifts, even with the color removed.

LOST IN THE LANDSCAPE

When walking through the garden, the tendency is to slow down and enjoy the finer details of a plant: things like delicate foliage, small blooms, soft textures or subdued colors. When a garden is viewed from a distance, however, many of these finer qualities become lost in the landscape, replaced by the garden's stronger features, such as bold color, visual balance and striking forms.

A black-and-white photograph taken from a distance will clearly show if this is happening in your garden. One way to prevent a plant from joining the missing-in-action list is to introduce a focal point near the disappearing plant to act as a beacon of sorts. This can be as easy as a bold-colored plant, one with a strong shape or even a garden ornament. By redirecting the line of sight back toward the disappearing plants, you've saved them from becoming visually extinct.

Another way to prevent the disappearing plant syndrome is to plant in drifts. Drifts, bands or large groupings of the same plant can create a bold statement in the garden when viewed both up close and far away.

While breathtaking when viewed up close, plants like bleeding hearts (*Dicentra spectabilis*), Russian sage (*Perovskia atriplicifolia*) or Japanese painted ferns (*Athyrium niponicum* var. *pictum*) can all but disappear in the garden when viewed from a distance. Planted in drifts, however, these delicate details develop more of a presence due to critical mass, allowing them to make an impact from all vantage points of a garden.

DESIGN SPOTLIGHT

JUST SAY "NO!" TO OFF-SEASONS

Before Remember, the best time to analyze your garden is when it's looking its worst! As this garden bed heads into winter, it's evident that a lack of contrast between colors, foliage shapes and plant forms is creating a less than exciting result. There are simply too many evergreen shrubs with tiny, round or variegated leaves.

After The addition of plants with contrasting heights, colors and foliage shapes provides interest throughout the winter months in this mild-climate garden bed.

BEFORE

AFTER

1. The deep wine colors of the plumbago (*Ceratostigma plumbaginoides*) echo the nearby colors of the mirror plant (*Coprosma repens* 'County Park Red') and the flowers of the *Grevillea* 'Superb'.

2. Orange sedge (*Carex testacea*) is not only evergreen in Zone 6 gardens, but it provides contrasting shape along with its warm colors.

3. A favorite of hummingbirds, this *Grevillea* 'Superb' explodes with colorful bottlebrush flowers most of the year. The shrub's upright form, combined with its large and feathery foliage, provides evergreen interest in Zone 9 gardens.

4. Hardy to Zone 2, stonecrop (*Sedum spurium* 'John Creech') not only acts as the mulch in this bed, it creates a lush effect, linking one area to another.

CIRCLE YOUR PLAN OF ACTION

Now that you've studied both color and black-and-white photographs of your garden, you've most likely identified several areas that could use some improvement. Congratulations—that's often the hardest part! Now you're ready to decide on your plan of action.

The next step is an easy one: Grab a permanent marker and begin circling the areas on the photographs that you'd like to improve. Don't worry about the specifics of how you'll fix these areas, as the solutions will become apparent as you continue reading this book. The point of this chapter is simply to help you identify your garden's troublesome spots. Now that you're armed with several ways to begin looking at your garden with fresh eyes, it's easy not only to discover any problem areas but, more importantly, to find the solutions to fix them.

While lush and green, this garden bed needs a bit of excitement to wake it up.

Drawing on the photo helps visualize where to insert interesting form, flowers and foliage color.

The pink and blue spheres of the hydrangeas and agapanthus contrast beautifully with the spiky ferns and gold and maroon foliage of surrounding plants.

FLOWERS

FORM

COLORFUL FOLIAGE

CHAPTER 2

COLOR

The creative use of color is one of the most powerful tools in your garden design toolbox. Whether tying together a disjointed garden, creating exciting optical illusions or breathing new life into your garden, learn how color can liberate your garden's glory. Visit www.hortmag.com/gardencolorwheel for a free colorwheel worksheet perfect for use in your garden.

Soft colors provided by the 'Sally Holmes' and 'Autumn Sunset' climbing roses, combined with an overflowing window box, create an inviting entrance to this courtyard garden

THE HEART OF THE GARDEN

While a garden's other layers, such as texture and form, are certainly instrumental to its overall design, color tends to be at the heart of every memorable garden. For example, when recalling the remarkable gardens that are firmly rooted in your memory, more often than not certain aspects of color come to mind. Remember spending a refreshing afternoon in the cool and sophisticated all-white garden? Or the warm shades of pumpkin, coral and gold in a garden that reminded you of the slanted sunlight of an autumn afternoon? Personally, whenever I see flowers with deep, rich magenta hues, my mind hears my grandmother's soft voice, proudly calling me over to see her prized peony's first bloom.

In addition to the personal "pull" of color, I can think of no other layer in the garden that is more powerful, with the ability to fix a wide range of common garden headaches. For example, if your garden has succumbed to one-of-each-itis (too many plants with no rhyme or reason), harmony can often be reinstated with the clever use of color. If your garden is uncomfortable during the hot days of summer, a colorful "sleight of hand" can help visually cool it down. Perhaps you wish you had a little more space in your small and cramped garden. Creating a colorful illusion can often be the answer to this common problem.

While colorful blooms are what we generally notice first in a spring and summer garden, what happens during the fall and winter seasons when flowers are scarce? To create a garden with year-round harmony, it's essential to include layers of color extending far beyond flowers: layers such as foliage, hardscaping, structures and even artwork. With the ability to conjure up memories, fix a wide range of everyday problems and carry your garden through the year, it's no wonder color is one of the most effective layers in the garden!

> To create a garden with year-round harmony, it's essential to include layers of color extending far beyond flowers: layers such as foliage, hardscaping, structures and even artwork.

THE COLOR WHEEL: YOUR GARDEN DESIGNER'S ASSISTANT

Color theory can sometimes be an intimidating and confusing concept to many gardeners. In an effort to bolster my clients' confidence with color, I used to encourage them by saying, "It's as easy as dressing yourself in the morning!" Then I started to notice what some people were wearing and realized I had been handing out some very bad advice. It's not always easy to understand which colors work (or don't work) together, and it's even trickier to know how to use them effectively in the garden.

While color theory can seem overwhelming, it's crucial to understand at least a few of the basic concepts. That's where the color wheel can help. In chapter one, I referred to your camera as your personal garden designer, so it's only fitting now to introduce you to your designer's new assistant: the color wheel. Once you understand how easy it is to use the wheel, you'll be able to begin waking up your weary garden!

In its simplest form, a color wheel is designed to demonstrate clearly which colors go with which. There are three *primary* colors that are as pure as they come (meaning they cannot be created by mixing any other colors together): yellow, blue and red. All other colors can be created by a combination of these three.

Next, there are three *secondary* colors: green, violet and orange. These colors are a result of mixing two primary colors together. These are spaced equal distance from one another, between the two primary colors from which they're created.

Finally, there are six *tertiary* (or *intermediate*) colors: yellow-green, blue-green, blue-violet, red-violet, red-orange and yellow-orange. These are colors achieved by a mixture of a primary color with its secondary hue.

From all of these colors, you can mix and match others in pleasing, harmonious combinations.

THE ABC'S OF THE COLOR WHEEL

A Is for Adjacent (a.k.a. Analogous Color Scheme)

Simply stated, analogous colors are adjacent to each other on the color wheel, usually in groups of three to six. The center color is generally used as the dominant color, while the surrounding colors are used to enrich the scheme.

Analogous colors tend to be the most harmonious to view since the colors used have components of each within them, therefore allowing them to blend seamlessly with one another. Be careful, though, as too many of the same analogous combinations in a garden can have a somewhat monotonous effect.

The analogous colors in this bed—blue, green and chartreuse—appear elegant and sophisticated.

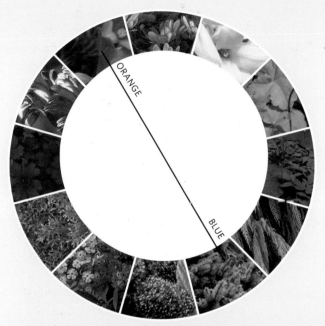

B is for Beyond
(a.k.a. Complementary Color Scheme)

Complementary colors, on the other hand, are those located opposite each other on the color wheel. This two-color combination is inherently high-contrast (and, therefore, high tension) and, as such, helps create a dynamic and energetic garden. For example, when a warm color such as orange is placed next to its direct opposite, a cool shade of blue, the combination commands the eye to stop and take notice, without having a jarring effect. If, on the other hand, that same orange was placed next to a bright color that wasn't quite its opposite on the color wheel (red-violet, for example) the result would still command the eye to take notice; however, it might be a bit unsettling.

When carefully chosen, complementary colors provide the visual punch a garden may need to wake it up. It is still important to use restraint when planting one complementary combination next to another, as you don't want the eye to work that hard. Instead, use plenty of analogous combinations in between the punches to allow the eye to rest and easily move along to the next grouping.

Oftentimes the most harmonious garden beds contain a mix of both analogous and complementary plant combinations.

Directly opposite one another on the color wheel, the vibrant blue of the salvia and the bright orange of the zinnias sing in perfect harmony.

DESIGN TIP

Yes, colors have temperatures! The color wheel not only clarifies the relationships of color with one another, but it illustrates the temperatures of colors, as well. Divide the wheel in half between violet and red-violet, straight across between yellow and yellow-green. You'll notice colors that appear cool are on one side (greens, blues and purples), and those that appear warm are on the other (yellows, oranges and reds).

C Is for Controlled Conflict
(a.k.a. Split-Complementary Color Scheme)

To create a garden with multiple layers of interest and color complexity, consider using a split-complementary color scheme. Simply put, this four-color combo consists of three analogous colors plus one complementary color, to introduce a carefully controlled visual punch to the garden bed while still remaining harmonious with its neighbors.

To determine which complementary color to use, find the point in the center of the color wheel where the three analogous colors meet. It's at that point that you continue drawing the center color's line, ending at the opposite side of the wheel. The complementary color to use in this color combination is where the line ends. When a complementary color is chosen this way, it provides dynamic contrast without the level of tension created by a two-color complementary color scheme.

Another benefit of using a split-complementary color scheme is the opportunity to gently introduce contrasting temperatures to the garden bed. For example, when combining a garden's red, orange and yellow colors (all warm tones) with the complementary (and cool) shades of purple, the mix of opposing temperatures adds yet another level of subtle complexity to the garden.

Adding temperature to the garden is an important step when deciding on the mood of your garden. For example, do you want a garden that will excite, energize and stimulate your creativity? Then consider introducing warm and hot colors into your garden. On the other hand, if a calm and relaxing space is what you desire, introducing the cooler shades of the color wheel will help you achieve that effect.

The red-hot flowers of the penstemon act as fireworks to wake up this soothing combination of dark green, light green and gray.

YELLOW-ORANGE

VIOLET

BLUE-VIOLET

BLUE

D Is for Ditto
(a.k.a. Monochromatic Color Scheme)

In a nutshell, a monochromatic color scheme sticks within a single color palette. While it is the simplest of all color schemes, it's also the most difficult to effectively translate in the garden. Not only is it challenging for most gardeners to stick within such a tight framework of color, but more importantly, a deeper understanding of color theory is also required in order to maintain harmony while avoiding monotony.

The use of monochromatic shades of red-violet create a serene atmosphere in this shady garden.

DESIGN TIP

Monochromatic doesn't have to mean monotonous! Just remember to periodically grab the eye's attention and hold it. To accomplish this within a single-color combination, first place the shade with the highest contrast (bright purple, for example) in a place where you want the eye to begin the journey (a.k.a. the focal point). Next, surround this focal point with softer shades of the same color, which give the eye a chance to slow down a bit before encountering the next area of high contrast. Remember, placing too many high-contrast shades next to one another is certainly a headache in the making, while placing too many similar shades together makes for an uninspired border.

For those wanting to create a monochromatic garden, a basic understanding of color is required. Technically speaking, the colors on the color wheel are referred to as *hues* (the purest form of the color). If white is added to a color, it's referred to as a *tint*. If gray is added, it's called a *tone*. And if black is added to a color, it's referred to as a *shade*.

The *shades* of a color range from lightest to darkest and is the most important quality to understand when creating a monochromatic garden. The creative use of a color's shade is the difference between a garden that's lackluster and one that's a masterpiece. A successful all-red border, for example, doesn't use just one shade of red (e.g., bright) but contains multiple shades, ranging from the lightest and softest all the way down to the deepest and darkest. It's this type of skillful combination that creates dynamic interest in a monochromatic garden, while simultaneously appearing serene and elegant.

TIME TO TAKE OFF THE TRAINING WHEELS

TURN A MISTAKE INTO A MASTERPIECE

When examining a garden bed that fizzles instead of flourishes, oftentimes the culprits are clashing colors. A quick glance at the color wheel will confirm if this is the case or not. For example, if the colors in question don't fall within an analogous, complementary, monochromatic or split-complementary color scheme, the color wheel can help pinpoint which offending color needs to be removed.

Color clashes are especially common among plants with multi-colored foliage. Unlike other planting combinations that require integrating only one or two foliage colors, when one of the plants happens to have multicolored leaves, it requires coordinating several colors at once. When doing this, it's important to remember that all of the colors in each leaf need to harmonize with their neighbors, not just one or two. Luckily, if a combination has gone awry, once the color wheel has helped identify the offending color, the solution might be as simple as swapping one plant with another.

FIND A REFEREE

But what happens when you discover the culprits of a troubled garden bed are clashing colors among large, established plants that you can't transplant? An easy solution borrowed from interior design can often solve the problem without having to uproot your plants. To restore harmony between two discordant plants, simply find a third plant that contains shades of both of the offending colors, and place it near the other two. This third plant acts as a visual referee, creating a common bond between the two clashing colors and breaking up a potentially chaotic grouping.

Referring to the color wheel, it's apparent that the multicolored foliage of the coprosma poses a problem with its neighbors. While the analogous blue color of the fescue harmonizes with the coprosma's green, it clashes with the other peach and orange tones.

The solution? Swapping the clashing blue fescue grass with the analogous green *Lomandra* results in a much more harmonious color combination.

DESIGN SPOTLIGHT

HELPING A SPRUCE AND AGAVE PLAY NICELY

Before This garden bed seems to be at war with itself. The main players, the blue spruce (*Picea pungens*)and the octopus agave, are fighting to determine this garden bed's design style (Asian vs. Southwestern), and the nearby hot and cold visual temperatures provide even more conflict. A quick glance at the color wheel shows that even though the blue and orange colors are complementary, they're also high tension. The excess visual tension in this garden bed, from both the opposing colors and conflicting design styles, has an unusually divisive effect.

After Removing the hot orange colors creates a restful feeling while the blue flowers of the Ground Morning Glory (*Convolvulus mauritanicus*) help to knit together the spruce and agave.

BEFORE

AFTER

1. The first step in restoring harmony is to remove the distracting and high-tension orange colors from the garden bed.

2. A few visual referees are needed to unite the two design styles, in this case, the colors blue and yellow. The focal point plant, octopus agave (*Agave vilmoriniana* 'Variegata'), contains both colors.

3. The color blue, pulled from the sparring spruce and agave, is echoed with pansies, Ground Morning Glory and echeverias to act as a rope, tying together the two opposing plants.

4. Warm shades of yellow (from the agave's stripes, abelia's foliage and bi-colored pansy) are woven throughout to act as another peacemaker in this planting combination.

DIRECT THE LINE OF SIGHT

Creating a garden can be compared to producing a play: The hardscaping is the set, the plants are the cast of characters and you're the director. As the director, you not only need the skills to visually tell a story, but you need to lead the audience from one scene to the next without them realizing they're being led. Color is one of the most important tools in your design arsenal.

For example, even though a garden may contain a pathway leading from point A to point B, that doesn't necessarily guarantee it will be used to explore the garden. Oftentimes a little-used pathway is the result of a lack of interest, with nothing to entice a visitor to discover what might lie beyond. One way to correct this problem is to place something at the end of the pathway to pique one's interest, to hint that something interesting lies beyond. That's where color comes in to play. Use a wow-factor color at the end of the pathway, or peeking around the corner, to catch one's eye and lead them down the path.

Just as important as leading a visitor toward a specific destination, color can help lead a visitor away from something as well, which is crucial when you have an eyesore lurking in the garden. Most gardens, no matter their size, have something in them—for example, an unsightly air-conditioning unit, an austere utility pole or a neighbor's looming roof line—trying to steal the attention away from the stars of the show. If you are not able to physically remove the eyesore from your garden, its impact can at least be minimized. The solution is often as simple as strategically placing a bold color away from the offending eyesore to redirect the line of sight toward a more appealing location.

The bold color of the Japanese maple beckons the visitor to further explore the garden.

The warm color of the burgundy fountain grass appears to move forward against the cool colors of the grasses and lavender. The result is a bed that looks deeper than it actually is.

CREATING OPTICAL ILLUSIONS WITH COLOR

Most memorable gardens have their fair share of everyday problems. However, through the use of optical illusions, these problems can discreetly disappear from sight. Color is an effective component in creating many of these optical illusions and, once mastered, is a highly effective way to begin the process of garden transformation.

EXPAND A SMALL SPACE

Deep garden beds are at the top of many gardeners' wish lists and for good reason. Creating beds that are lush, colorful and filled with varying heights is much easier to do when you have plenty of space in which to use a wide selection of plants. Unfortunately, many gardens just don't have the room for deep garden beds and are filled, instead, with narrow and sometimes awkward spaces. One of the pitfalls of a skinny garden bed is the lack of space to include multiple layers of plants, and as such, it appears visually flat and two-dimensional.

Luckily, the illusion of a much deeper garden bed can easily be created through the manipulation of color. As mentioned earlier, when divided in half, the color wheel represents both cool and warm temperatures. In addition to temperature, these same colors also represent movement: cool colors (green through purple) are referred to as visually *passive*, while warm colors (yellow through red) are visually *active*.

This concept is crucial in a skinny garden bed as active, warm colors give the illusion of moving forward, while passive, cool colors appear to recede. When the eye perceives movement, it translates that into depth.

DESIGN TIP

Another benefit of introducing warm colors among cool ones (and vice versa) is the visual tension created and the effect it has on a visitor's eye. If the majority of a garden's colors fall within one temperature range, the tendency is to cast a cursory glance over the garden. By mixing temperatures throughout the garden, the tension causes the eye to naturally slow down, allowing one to take in all the subtleties the garden has to offer.

RESTORE VISUAL BALANCE

In addition to creating the illusion of movement, plants with certain colors can also appear to have visual *weight*, seeming lighter or heavier than their surrounding neighbors. Regardless of a plant's size, colors that are dark, warm and intense appear much heavier than their light, cool and muted counterparts. If that dark-colored plant happens to have substantial size, then it will appear heavier yet. An even distribution of visual weight in the garden is essential as it helps to create harmony through its symmetry.

When examining the photographs of your garden (as discussed in chapter one), check to see if it appears balanced or not. Most often, gardens that are out of balance are the result of beds of uneven size and shape. For example, the larger bed naturally contains more plants than the smaller, resulting in a visually unbalanced space. While an obvious solution might be to balance the other side with an equal number of plants, when the beds are of uneven size this isn't always possible. To tip the scales back to center, use a more creative approach to create the *illusion* of balance. If, for example, one side of the garden has wider and deeper beds, strategically place one or two plants with dark, weighty colors on the opposite side to help redistribute the visual weight. If those dark plants are of substantial size, the impact will be even greater.

The two garden beds flanking the staircase are uneven in size and depth, with the potential to create visual imbalance. The strategic placement of the large burgundy Japanese maple in the upper left corner helps tip the visual scale back to center.

The dark burgundy sedum appears much heavier than the surrounding silver plants, even though it's a much smaller size.

CHANGE YOUR GARDEN'S MOOD

Most gardens are a personal reflection of their creators: a combination of personality, artistic tendencies, collections, hobbies and interests. Unfortunately, though, many times a gardener may not feel any personal connection to his or her garden. This is most often the result of a mismatch in personalities; for example, a serious and contemplative person will undoubtedly feel disconnected from his buoyant and light-hearted garden.

Yes, your garden has personalities and moods just like we all do. Some gardens have a cheery personality with a sunny disposition; others are mellow or serious, while many can be a pleasing combination of both. If you and your garden are mismatched, the solution to bring you both together again can often be as simple as rethinking your garden's colors.

While it may seem a little intimidating to determine which colors best represent who you are, the answers are most likely already around you.

Look around your home to see what colors you use most often. Or take a look at your wardrobe to find the colors you generally wear. Do you gravitate toward earth tones, pastels or jewel tones? It probably won't take you long to figure out what colors you tend to use, and from there, you can decide whether you want to continue this thread in your garden or take a detour and try something new.

This black and gray monochromatic border can be compared to a melodramatic teenager.

On the other hand, the bright orange, yellow and pink colors in this garden are similar to a perky cheerleader.

DESIGN TIP

Many believe in the therapeutic qualities certain colors contain, helping to influence one's state of mind, feelings and moods. Due to their dramatic effect, plants with specific colors are used strategically by gardeners hoping to achieve a specific desired result.

- Yellows indicate fun, humor and personal power.
- Oranges stimulate creativity and represent hope and happiness.
- Reds increase physical energy and represent passion and stability.
- Purples stimulate imagination and represent respect and artistic talent.
- Blues increase calmness and inner peace.
- Greens represent balance, hope and harmony.

ADJUST YOUR GARDEN'S THERMOSTAT

The color wheel indicates a color's warm or cool temperatures, but did you know that, when used in the garden, these colors have a direct *physical* effect on a person? Just by looking at a hot-colored (or cool-colored) garden bed, the mind registers it as either a few degrees warmer or cooler than in reality.

This is a remarkably successful illusion to manipulate the perceived temperature of your garden. For example, if you garden in a zone with exceptionally hot summers, consider using plants in refreshing shades of blue, purple, white and green. On the other hand, if your garden is generally a chilly place to be (regardless of the season), incorporating warm shades of orange, red and yellow will give the illusion of warmth. This is especially effective in a garden's cooler, shady corners, as the warm colors will act as the missing sunshine.

The fluffy white clouds, cool blue water and dark purple lupine are the epitome of a refreshing color combination.

To remind this homeowner of a cool vacation at the lake, she filled a sunny border with similar shades of blue, purple and white.

The golden glow of yellow, peach and orange turn up the heat in this sunny border.

Introducing silver into the garden can have a calming effect

SHADES OF GRAY

The color gray (or silver) straddles the line between both hot and cold temperatures, with the power to change a garden's visual temperature in either direction. As a result, pay particular attention to the colors that surround gray, as you may inadvertently create an overly hot and glaring garden when your intent may have been to cool it down.

For example, light-colored hardscaping (such as a cement sidewalk or pavers in pale shades) can appear blindingly bright in the hot summer sun. The effect is intensified when silver- or gray-colored plants are used near this hardscaping. To visually reduce the glare and temperature of this bed, surround the silver-colored plants with others in darker and cooler shades, such as green, purple or blue.

Introducing silver into the garden can have a calming effect as well, allowing a pause in the color scheme, a place for the eye to rest. Often referred to as a transitional color, silver is especially effective when blending a hot-colored garden bed with a nearby cool-colored bed.

Use caution when pairing silver and gray together, as the result might be an uncomfortably bright combination.

Swapping the fescue's bright silver with the sedge's refreshing green brings down the visual temperature of this combination.

DESIGN SPOTLIGHT

It's hard to enjoy your garden when the temperatures outside are soaring. One way to counter-balance the oppressive heat is to create an illusion of coolness and tranquility. In an effort to entice visitors to explore the garden, despite the summer's heat, refreshing colors such as dark green, icy blue, deep purple and pure white are used to create a visually cooler environment. An added illusion is one of cool and shady shadows as a result of the high contrast (and movement) between the bright silver and the dark green.

1. The antique water pump is the perfect garden ornament for this hot bed, representing cool and refreshing water.

2. The flowers of the 'Hawkshead' fuchsia resemble falling raindrops.

3. The deep purple blooms of the heliotrope add a pop of refreshing color to the cool tones of this garden bed.

4. The name of this euphorbia says it best— 'Glacier Blue'—and further helps to reduce the visual temperature.

COLOR ECHOES: TAKING IT UP A NOTCH

In addition to the practical problem-solving abilities of color, it's also one of the easiest ways to begin adding harmony back into your garden. When thoughtfully used, color acts as a beautiful ribbon, weaving throughout the garden and tying seemingly disparate elements together. This is most often accomplished through the use of color repetition.

The easiest, and perhaps most obvious, way to repeat color is to use the same plant, mixed in here and there, throughout the garden. A more creative way to introduce color repetition throughout the garden, however, is through the creation of color echoes. In its simplest form, a color echo is a combination of colors (bold, subtle or a mix of both) that have elements of one another contained within each of them.

One of the easiest ways to begin experimenting with color echoes is by using a combination of plants with flowers within a similar color family. Remember, a color echo uses subtle *hints* of the same color, not necessarily using only the *same* color.

The more you experiment with creating color echoes with flowers, the more you'll become aware of that flower's other sources of color. For example, while the petals of a flower may be the first (and most obvious) color to come to mind, look a little deeper, and you may notice other colors coming from different parts of the flower, such as the flower's center, stamens and seed heads or a petal's subtle shading. These other, less obvious, colors are a golden opportunity to begin creating a little visual magic in your garden.

The yellow stripe of the 'Pinstripe' petunia pops when planted next to the bright foliage of creeping Jenny (*Lysimachia nummularia* 'Aurea').

Opposite page, top: Close examination of the coneflower reveals two colors to consider in a color echo: pink from the petals and burnt orange from the center.

Bottom: The vibrant red stamens of this cold-hardy kahili ginger lily (*Hedychium gardnerianum*) offer a unique color echo opportunity.

LOOKING BEYOND THE FLOWER

Flowers are fleeting while foliage is forever! This may be a slight exaggeration, but don't forget the other elements of a plant that provide many months of color in your garden. Creating color combinations with flowers is certainly fun and easy, though using the other features of a plant to create *complex echoes* is often more rewarding. As you experiment with complex color echoes, you'll end up with longer-lasting interest in the garden that can be stunning in its subtlety.

FOLIAGE

No other element of a plant offers more opportunities for creating complex color echoes than foliage. In addition to working with multicolored, bi-colored, or single-colored leaves, there are many other aspects of foliage to consider. For example, look under the leaves for hidden, and often brilliant, colors.

Or consider using the color of a plant's new growth to incorporate throughout your garden bed. Many varieties of nandinas, peonies, roses, pieris or photinias, for example, are tipped with bright, garnet-colored leaves each spring as their new growth emerges. Highlight this unexpected burst of color with surrounding plants in similar shades to make an impressive statement in the spring garden.

In addition to a plant's new growth, consider a plant's old growth as well. Fall's fiery colors are a welcome sight in the garden, signaling the end of the gardening season and a time to rest. With a little planning, highlight this much-anticipated show of color by coordinating it with late-blooming flowers and other similarly colored foliage.

Since gardens are an organic and ever-changing form of living art, having seasonal color echoes pop up throughout different times of the year is nothing short of magical.

The chocolate and raspberry colors of this peony's new foliage welcomes spring's arrival, adding a much-needed burst of color to an awakening landscape.

Peach echoes wind throughout this bed, resulting from the foliage of *Heuchera* 'Peach Flambé', snapdragon flowers and the bracts and stems of the wood spurge (*Euphorbia amygdaloides* 'Purpurea').

The deep maroon foliage of the *Weigela* 'Dark Horse' harmonizes beautifully with the pink, lavender and white blooms of sweet William (*Dianthus barbatus*).

The vibrant fall colors of the crape myrtle highlight the late-season blooms of this hydrangea and *Grevillea* 'Superb'; they are further echoed by the brilliant foliage of the Nandina 'Moon Bay'.

UNUSUAL SOURCES OF COLOR

Creating complex color echoes using a plant's flowers and foliage is one of the most common, yet rewarding, ways to begin weaving color throughout your garden. Study a plant a little longer, and you'll begin to notice many other elements from which to pull unusual colors. Elements such as a plant's stems, berries, seed heads and even bark are less common, but no less important, opportunities to create an unusual color echo. When using echoes from these less obvious sources of subtle color, harmony is achieved, elevating your garden to new heights.

Another benefit of these uncommon sources of color is that many are either seasonal (such as berries and seed heads) or year-round (such as stems and bark), providing many more months of interest in the garden. When color is pulled from these longer-lasting elements, your garden's harmony will last throughout the year.

Stems

Many times the stems of a plant are a shade lighter or darker than its foliage or flower (for example, 'Matrona' sedum or *Hebe* 'Anomala') and, as such, are opportunities to begin introducing darker (or lighter) shades of a color into your garden.

In addition, certain varieties of shrubs (such as 'Cardinal' dogwood or 'Sango-kaku' Japanese maple) turn brilliant shades of red and gold in chilly winter temperatures. These colorful stems offer much-needed interest to a bleak winter garden and can be further echoed with nearby artwork, structures or other winter-hardy elements.

Berries

Seasonal berries offer yet another opportunity for creating complex color echoes in the garden. The brilliant yellow berries of the yellow-fruited American holly (*Ilex opaca* 'Xanthocarpa')

Imagine the deep pink stems of the sedum 'Matrona' surrounded with flowers in similar shades of rose for a complex color echo.

Pairing the black stems of cow parsley (*Anthriscus sylvestris* 'Ravenswing') with the dark foliage of the *Angelica gigas* creates an unexpected complex color echo.

brighten up a fading summer garden, especially when surrounded by other late-blooming perennials such as goldenrod (*Solidago*) or sneezeweed (*Helenium*). And what better way to usher in the fall season than with the cherry-red berries of mountain ash (*Sorbus aucuparia*) or Cardinal Candy (*Viburnum dilatatum* 'Henneke')?

Edibles

Whether due to limited sunshine, shrinking garden spaces, or the desire to grow your own food, mixing edibles and ornamentals together in a garden bed makes perfect sense. Besides the practical reasons of growing your own food, many gardeners grow edibles purely for aesthetic purposes. With more and more colorful heirloom varieties available each year, the opportunities to create imaginative color echoes using edibles are seemingly endless.

Many gardeners hesitate to incorporate edibles within their ornamental garden beds for fear of the unsightly appearance of many late-season vegetables. While this may be true for some edibles (such as tomatoes and squash), there are many others that remain tidy, colorful and healthy throughout the season. For example, consider pairing the yellow-splashed leaves of the compact 'Icterina' sage with the lime green foliage of lady's mantle (Alchemilla mollis). The dwarf 'Fairy Tale' eggplant, with its velvety-green leaves, inky purple stems and jewel-toned purple blooms, would make a stunning combination with a neighboring alum root (Heuchera 'Obsidian') or the whirling butterfly-blooms of a compact Gaura lindheimeri 'Belleza Dark Pink'. Don't forget the many shades of maroon, lavender and white that long-lasting kale has to offer. The next time you visit your nursery, consider edibles as another way to introduce unusual color echoes throughout your garden.

The late summer berries of the beautyberry shrub (*Callicarpa americana*) are sure to brighten up any garden, especially when surrounded with plants that contain similar shades of magenta.

The kale's mauve-colored ribs create a complex color echo when combined with the annual blooms of nemesia 'Bluebird' and the soft pink flowers of the climbing 'Cécile Brunner' rose.

Without the icy blue foliage of the fescue, the unusual colors of the stones might very well be lost in the landscape.

The flagstone's many shades of maroon, rust and brown are echoed in the garden bed with the surrounding foliage and flowers.

Hardscaping

Instead of focusing on using color echoes from plants alone, don't forget that your garden consists of so much more. To see what I mean, take a step back and look at your garden as a whole, not only consisting of plants, but also hardscaping, nearby structures and accessories (such as containers and art). Harmony is achieved when all of the individual players in your garden have common, yet distinct, threads that stitch them together, resulting in a stunning and colorful tapestry.

Creating color echoes with plants is often the first of many layers within this tapestry. In fact, this colorful layer is often considered the foundation of your garden, upon which all other layers are built. Coordinating your plant echoes with nearby hardscaping is yet one more layer to add to your garden's complex color scheme.

Hardscaping is generally thought of as the hard, solid and non-moveable areas of your garden, such as patios, stone walls, pathways, fences and fireplaces. More often than not, hardscaping is made of natural materials (such as wood, brick, flagstone, gravel and stone) and, as such, is likely to blend seamlessly within your garden.

In addition to adding another colorful layer within your garden, hardscaping is a key player in providing year-round interest. Hardscaping tends to act more as a backdrop during the exuberant months of summer, when the spotlight shines bright on your planting combinations. In the stark days of winter, though, hardscaping takes center stage. This seasonal exposure is all the more reason to highlight these hardworking, yet often overlooked, elements of your garden by including them as part of your garden's color echoes.

Stone Whether stones are used to create a rustic wall, to border a garden bed, or to direct one's attention as a strategically placed focal point, their color should always be taken into consideration as part of a color echo. Stones not only highlight the color echoes of nearby plants, but the reverse is true, as well. If a stone contains a particularly stunning color that you don't want to go unnoticed, consider using the color of nearby plants to redirect the spotlight back on the stone.

Gravel Gravel is generally used throughout the garden in larger quantities than individual stones, taking the form of meandering pathways or providing the surface for casual seating areas. As such, depending on the color chosen, its mass can either be harmonious with the surrounding garden or it can stick out like a sore thumb.

Just as plants have visual temperatures, hardscaping does, as well. Special attention needs to be given to the color of gravel to avoid inadvertently raising or lowering the temperature in your garden. For example, if you've chosen gravel with colors in the cool shades (with gray and blue tones) and you surround it with plants with similar colors, the temperature will visually be reduced. This might be a desirable effect in a hot climate but not the best thing for colder areas. Conversely, light-colored gravel with tan and peach tones, combined with plants in similarly warm colors, will raise the visual temperature.

The burnt caramel colors of *Heuchera* 'Peach Flambé' foliage harmonize with the nearby stones bordering the garden bed.

When shopping for gravel, bring home as many samples as you can to see first-hand what they'll look like in your garden's setting. Group them on a white piece of paper to see their true colors without other color distractions. If other hardscape materials will be used in your garden, place the gravel on a sample of it, as well, to see whether or not the colors harmonize with one another.

The combination of the warm colors of the brick with the peachy tones of the 'Oregon Sunset' Japanese maple create an inviting entryway near this home's front door.

The tile wall's vibrant coral, orange and black colors are echoed in the nearby rose and water fountain.

Brick The warm, earthy shades of terra cotta, red, orange or tan contained within bricks provide an opportunity to create warm and inviting color echoes in your garden. As with other hardscaping options, surrounding bricks with plants in similar warm colors will visually warm up an area in the garden. To provide a welcome contrast or to cool down a color scheme, surround the bricks with plants in colors from the cool side of the color wheel.

Wood Whether stained, painted or left untouched, hardscaping made with wood can offer endless color echoes in the garden, from brightly colored statements to subtle, elegant whispers. For classic yet rustic charm, it's hard to beat an arbor painted white, accented with the white blooms of a climbing rose. Wood is also an opportunity to bring out the hidden artist in you, allowing you to experiment with exciting, bold colors in the garden with minimal expense and commitment. At the end of the day, if you decide you just can't live with your newly painted fire-engine red trellis, you can easily change the color.

Keep in mind that wooden structures in the garden require regular maintenance and will need periodic repainting and re-staining to look their best.

Accessories and Structures Finally, don't forget about the many accessories in your garden, such as artwork, containers, birdbaths, fountains and outdoor furniture, as yet one more opportunity to continue your garden's color scheme. Separate structures (whether for fun or function) include potting sheds, garden nooks, greenhouses and any other type of freestanding building in the garden. These structures tend to be prominent in the garden, requiring special attention be given to their style and appearance. Whether they are painted in complementary or analogous colors, adding this final layer to the complex color echoes you've created will wake up the weariest of gardens.

Colorful patio furniture highlight the nearby chartreuse foliage and flowers of the creeping Lysimachia (L. *procumbens* 'Aurea') and wild sunflower (*Inula helenium*).

The burgundy trim of this potting shed is echoed with the foliage and flowers of the nearby Japanese painted fern (*Athyrium niponicum* var. *pictum*) and cranesbill geranium (*G. phaeum* 'Samobor').

The softly faded color of the lamppost blends seamlessly with the variegated foliage and flowers nestled beneath it.

Perfect harmony is achieved through color echoes that weave throughout the foliage of *Oxalis* 'Sunset Velvet', the terra-cotta container and the brick patio.

CHAPTER

3

TEXTURE

The *Sunning Nude* sculpture by Elizabeth Rose lounges among the soft and wispy grasses, perfectly capturing the sensuality of texture.

There's no doubt about it—texture is an alluring element in the garden, creating an irresistible physical reaction among kids and adults alike. Who can resist the uncontrollable urge to stroke the soft leaf of a lamb's ear, or run a hand along the peeling bark of a paperbark maple? Texture is also a design workhorse, able to solve a wide range of everyday garden problems.

TOUCH, SIGHT AND SOUND: TEXTURE'S THREE SENSES

Gardening appeals to all of our senses: touch, sight, smell, sound and taste. Part of what makes a particular garden so memorable is its creative use of layers, with each having its own sensory appeal. Texture is often a subtle, yet powerful, element in a harmonious garden, and when thoughtfully used, it can appeal to three senses—sight, sound and touch.

The adjectives used to describe a plant's texture often hint at its usefulness in the garden and to which sense it might appeal. For example, plant textures appealing to sight might contain words such as *delicate*, *thick*, *dusky*, *shiny* or *airy* in their descriptions. These sight-oriented textures can be best used to make a strong visual impact in the garden, such as placing the shiny foliage of a mirror plant (*Coprosma repens*) near the matte leaves of carpet bugle (*Ajuga reptans*).

On the other hand, plant textures appealing to touch might use descriptors such as *velvety*, *knobby*, *fuzzy*, *prickly*, *rough* or *smooth*, and are best used to create a specific tactile experience in the garden. To encourage physical interaction in the garden, place these plants near the front of the border or along pathways where they're most likely to be touched.

But how does texture appeal to our sense of sound? Not only do certain textural plants contribute to our sense of hearing (the sound of wispy grasses or thick palm fronds rustling in the wind), but the textures of certain hardscaping materials can also create remarkably distinct audible experiences. For example, a rustic, country garden comes to mind when hearing the satisfying sound of nubby, gravel crunching underfoot; or a feeling of formality comes over you when you hear the sharp echoes of polished granite. As elusive as they may be, textural sounds are no less important in creating some of the most subtle, yet impactful, layers in the garden.

Texture is often a subtle, yet powerful, element in a harmonious garden

The bold, thick, leathery leaves of the *Rodgersia* 'Bronze Peacock' appear to be made of metal.

The cotton-ball puffs of the harestail grass (*Lagurus ovatus*) beg to be touched.

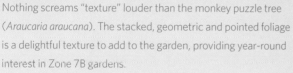

Nothing screams "texture" louder than the monkey puzzle tree (*Araucaria araucana*). The stacked, geometric and pointed foliage is a delightful texture to add to the garden, providing year-round interest in Zone 7B gardens.

The dark colors of the finely cut foliage of Black Lace elderberry (*Sambucus nigra* 'Eva') provides a wispy backdrop for its delicate clusters of airy pink flowers.

The thick and deeply serrated foliage of the blue hesper palm (*Brahea armata*) provides textural interest as well as sound, as the palm fronds gently clap together in the wind.

The golden, fuzzy pompoms of the acacia tree's flowers, combined with the delicate tracery of the foliage are a visual and textural delight.

USING TEXTURE IN THE GARDEN

Identifying the adjectives that describe texture is one thing, but knowing how to use textures in the garden is another. Unsure of what to do, many people overuse a familiar texture with unintended and undesirable results. For example, an overuse of fine textures can result in disappearing plants or lackluster gardens; whereas, an overabundance of coarse and rough plants can create an oppressive, claustrophobic space. Luckily, a thorough understanding of texture and how to use it can easily prevent these common mistakes.

FOCAL POINTS

Heavily textured, bold foliage rivals the showiest of blooms. They are exciting, in-your-face attention grabbers that beg to be the focal point of a garden bed. Too many placed in a small area can look overly chaotic, however, but one or two placed strategically can become the shining stars of your garden.

SUPPORTING CAST

I often think of a garden as a spectacular theatrical performance, filled with highs and lows, lots of dramatic twists and various stars that make their appearance throughout the year. Along this line, finely textured plants often function as a play's supporting cast, helping those heavily textured drama queens stand out from the crowd. For example, to help shine the spotlight on the big, bold leaves of an artichoke plant, consider surrounding it with the lacy foliage of threadleaf coreopsis (*Coreopsis verticillata* 'Moonbeam') or the wispy blades of a Berkeley sedge (*Carex divulsa*). On the other hand, those same heavily textured plants can help wake up a garden planted with an excess of finely textured plants.

WINTER INTEREST

While deciduous plants may be resting during winter's cold months, other elements of the garden take their turn in the spotlight. Texture is at the heart of this winter show, including interesting bark of trees, a grass's tawny inflorescence and many highly structural and textural dried seedpods.

PROPORTION

Like most things in life, if a little is good, a lot isn't necessarily better. Proportion is vital to a garden's harmony, especially when using fine-textured plants in the garden. A general rule of thumb is to use one-third fine-textured to two-thirds coarse-textured plants to maintain enough contrast without visually tipping the scales in one direction or the other.

PLACEMENT

If you wish to use just one or two finely textured plants, consider planting them along the front of the border or in a container on the patio where their intricate details can be best appreciated up close. Keep the plants with bolder foliage placed farther back in the garden bed since they're easily appreciated from a distance.

DRIFTS

If you decide to place delicate textures further back in the garden, prevent their disappearing act by using a single variety grouped together in drifts. The mass created by drifts (or swaths) will have a greater visual impact in the garden, allowing fine textures to be appreciated from afar. Drifts of a similar texture also help to add a sense of order to the garden, keeping a gardener's ever-expanding plant palette in check.

BINDERS

Drifts of fine textures have a magnificent ethereal effect, similar to clouds, and they can softly fill the negative space in between larger, bolder plantings. These drifts act as a binder, of sorts, tying together separate areas of the garden with a cohesive and orderly flow.

Even though the purple smoke tree (*Cotinus coggygria* 'Royal Purple') is imposing in size, its soft, cloud-like blooms create a graceful and ethereal atmosphere in the garden.

The contrast of coarse and fine foliage allows each plant's qualities to brightly shine in this garden bed.

The delicate flowers and thin, strappy foliage of the *Crocosmia* 'Lucifer' have a much bigger visual impact when planted in drifts.

DESIGN TIP

A Moonlight Garden takes advantage of night's lack of light to heighten and tantalize the senses. Plants most appreciated under the light of a full moon include those with smooth, reflective foliage such as *Hosta fortunei* 'Albo-marginata' or *Coprosma repens* 'Marble Queen'. Take it one step further and choose plants that serve double duty with smooth foliage and shiny white flowers (many of which have a heavenly scent) such as *Camellia japonica* 'Alba Plena' or *Dicentra spectabilis* 'Alba'.

CONTRAST VS. REPETITION

Within a harmonious garden bed, you'll notice the different layers of color, texture, shape and form performing a delicate dance involving various ratios of contrast and repetition. On one hand, repetition is vital to maintaining a garden's consistency, preventing it from appearing random and chaotic. On the other hand, too much repetition makes a garden appear predictable and somewhat boring. Place too many fuzzy plants together, for example, and the texture's impact is lost. However, by placing a contrasting texture nearby (such as shiny or polished), the impact of the fuzzy texture is heightened. This use of a contrasting texture helps to wake up the combination, adding a jolt of excitement where least expected.

WHEN IN DOUBT, TAKE THE COLOR OUT

How do you know if your garden has the right ratios of repetition and contrast? This is where your camera can help. When looking at your planting combination, if it still doesn't look quite right, take a photo of it and remove the color (discussed in chapter one). Remember, photos let you look at a garden while *away* from the garden, allowing you to be more objective in your decision-making by essentially removing all distractions. By removing the color, you've eliminated the biggest distraction of all.

Your black-and-white photo will quickly point out if the contrast and repetition ratios are out of balance. Too much repetition and the plants will blend together into a single, unimaginative mass. Too little and the combination looks overly busy, with no place for the eye to rest before moving on to the next grouping.

The combination of fuzzy, lacy and smooth foliage creates a dynamic, yet serene, composition.

Opposite page, top: What causes this salvia and Heuchera combination to appear a little lackluster? Remove the color and the answer becomes clear; the culprit here is an overuse of fine-textured foliage and flowers.

Opposite page, middle: The textural contrast in this combination clearly shines through in both the color and black-and-white photographs.

Opposite page, bottom: Even with the color removed, this combination remains dynamic, despite the repetition of foliage textures. Strong contrasting colors are what allow each plant to brightly shine next to its neighbor.

TEXTURAL TAPESTRY

The soothing greens and blues in this analogous color combination are anything but monotonous, thanks to the masterful mix of contrasting textures found in the garden of Freeland and Sabrina Tanner. The textures from plants, as well as garden furniture and crunchy gravel, all contribute to this dynamic composition.

1. The slender, arching and toothy foliage of the terrestrial-looking pinwheel (*Puya venusta*) is clearly the focal point in this vignette. It not only provides visual interest but motion as well, reminding one of spinning pinwheels in the garden.

2. The garden furniture's sleek and polished metal is a pleasing contrast to both the crunchy, knobby gravel underfoot and the border's rough and rustic wooden texture.

3. The bold and puckered foliage of the *Hosta* 'Eola Sapphire' contrasts with the smaller, smoother leaves of the *Hosta* 'Patriot' planted at its feet.

4. The cottony, tight balls of the cold-hardy sedum (*Sempervivum arachnoideum*) look as if they're covered with cobwebs.

CREATING OPTICAL ILLUSIONS WITH TEXTURE

When used to its full capacity, texture is an impressive element in the garden, able to effortlessly combine sensuality with practicality. But did you realize texture is also a key factor in creating optical illusions in the garden? Similar to color (discussed in chapter two), with a little textural know-how, you can learn how to transform many of your garden's everyday problems through the use of optical illusions.

GIVE YOUR GARDEN BREATHING ROOM

It seems the trend these days are larger homes placed too close to one another, with smaller and smaller spaces in which to create a garden. Unfortunately, this often results in a cramped and claustrophobic atmosphere. Just because a garden is small doesn't mean it must take a back seat to one that's expansive. In fact, many times it's easier to appreciate the intricate details of a garden that's manageable in size.

One way to help restore harmony to a small, oppressive garden is to use the textural qualities of plants to create a cozy, open and airy illusion. To do this, minimize the use of bold and highly textured plants, and instead, use a higher ratio of plants with light and delicate textures. It's hard to breathe when you're in a small space filled with oversized and heavily ridged gunnera leaves, the monster-size foliage of banana plants or thick and deeply lobed palm fronds. Instead, fill your garden with wispy grasses, trees with small and shiny leaves, and perennials with needle-like or lacy foliage and flowers. Once the eye sees light and space through these finely textured plants, the mind interprets the space as a relaxing, airy and open garden.

This ultra-skinny space not only controls the invasive horsetail (*Equisetum hyemale*), but the drift helps to emphasize the plant's finer details.

The combination of small, smooth and shiny leaves of the boxwood, ivy and pittosporum creates an open and airy atmosphere in this small courtyard garden.

TRANSFORM A SMALL GARDEN INTO A LARGER ONE

In addition to transforming a cramped garden into a spacious one, the creative use of texture can also help give the illusion of greater depth. For example, small, feathery and wispy textures (such as many ferns, bamboo, deadnettle or lavender) tend to visually recede into the background, whereas plants with bolder and more textured foliage (hostas, rodgersias or bergenias, for example) tend to visually advance.

To create this optical illusion in a narrow space, place bold and highly textured plants in front of a border, with the finely textured plants in the back. Voilà! The mind and eye will automatically see this space as much deeper than it actually is.

TURN ON THE LIGHTS

Small spaces tend to lack natural light due to overgrown shrubs, towering trees, tall fences and tightly packed second-story homes. The missing sunlight, unfortunately, causes a small space to feel even smaller.

To help brighten these dark spaces, increase your garden's natural light by using shiny, polished and reflective textures. Plants with mirror-like foliage (such as laurel, holly, magnolias, coprosmas or periwinkle) literally reflect the natural light and help make a small space seem brighter. In addition to plants, don't forget about the texture of hardscaping, such as patios and pathways. Reflective materials such as smooth flagstone and polished granite also create the illusion of additional light.

Planting bold leaves in the front of the border, with smaller leaves behind, helps create an illusion of depth in this otherwise narrow garden bed.

The delicate Japanese forest grass (*Hakonechloa macra* 'Aureola') nestles with the bold foliage of the comfrey (*Symphytum* × *uplandicum* 'Axminster Gold'), creating a visually warm combination with plenty of textural contrast.

DESIGN TIP

Bright yellow and chartreuse colors act as the missing sunshine in shady gardens, giving the illusion of brightness and warmth. Just remember to use a higher ratio of fine textures to bold to keep the space looking open and airy.

CREATE THE ILLUSION OF INTIMACY

Large gardens placed in expansive settings often have their own set of challenges. These spaces can appear overwhelming and the eye doesn't know quite where to begin. This is especially common when a garden is surrounded by acres and acres of natural beauty. The eye automatically looks to the mountain range (or ocean, prairie or forest) with the garden never quite getting its due attention.

There are a few challenges in a garden such as this, the first being how to direct the attention back to the garden. Focal points are instrumental in directing the eye, and as mentioned earlier, plants with bold and highly textured foliage are excellent at accomplishing this task. It's not easy to cast a dismissive glance at a giant butterbur (*Petasites japonicus*) or elephant ear (*Colocasia* spp.)!

Once the attention is brought back to the garden, another challenge is to keep it there. The creative use of highly textured foliage is just one of many ways to keep one's interest firmly rooted in the garden. But remember, too many high-contrast plants used together can quickly result in a hectic-looking garden. To avoid this, it is essential to use plenty of fine textures not only to fill in the spaces between the high-contrast plants but also to give the eye a chance to rest again before encountering the next grouping of plants.

Finally, as a result of too much space, large gardens can end up looking a bit distant and impersonal. Intimate spaces need to be created within the garden to visually bring a large space down to scale again. Larger plants with bold and coarse textures (such as viburnum, rhododendron or magnolias) are particularly effective in creating the illusion of intimacy, as they can visually stand up to the expansive space surrounding them.

The oversized leaves of the butterbur (*Petasites japonicus*) stand out in this very large garden, helping to create a sense of intimacy in an otherwise expansive space.

Opposite page: The bold foliage of the cold-hardy century plant (*Agave americana*, USDA Zones 8–12) holds its own against the spectacular rolling hillsides of Sonoma, California. The wispy blades of the grasses combined with the needle-like foliage of nearby rosemary provide a soft and welcome contrast. This garden was created by James van Sweden and Sheila Brady of Oehme, van Sweden & Assoc.

This bold, finely toothed sago palm adds a tropical effect to this Zone 6 Connecticut garden. The wheeled container allows this palm (hardy in Zones 8-12) to be moved indoors to overwinter.

CHANGE YOUR GARDEN'S LOCALE

When designing a garden, it's important to remember to embrace and celebrate the climate and area in which you live, something designers call a *sense of terroir*. This phrase has its roots in winemaking and is roughly translated as recognizing the individual characteristics of a vineyard's climate, soil and topography that directly influence the nuances of the wine. In garden design, sense of terroir is often interpreted as sense of *place*; it's having your garden reflect the specific region and its environmental factors in which you live. For example, if you live in a hot and arid desert environment, why not celebrate your region's diversity by planting cactus, succulents and other drought-tolerant plants instead of trying to force water-thirsty and fragile plants to survive.

Metaphorically speaking, a sense of place can have an entirely different meaning. Instead of the literal translation of the words "the place," they can also refer to the place in your memory to which you want your garden to transport you. Perhaps this place is a sentimental garden of your childhood, a magical garden from your travels or a garden that has the look and feel of your place of origin. Some of the most memorable gardens are those that combine both the literal and metaphorical definitions of place.

If you long for a garden that transports you to another part of the world, it can be tricky finding plants that are regionally appropriate and will have a fighting chance in your garden's climate. One solution is to use the different qualities of plants to create the illusion of being in an entirely different region. Texture is one of a plant's main qualities that are remarkably effective in helping you achieve this illusion.

For example, many plants growing naturally in the tropics have oversized bold and coarse-textured foliage (just think of cannas, palm trees, angel's trumpets or banana plants).

The deeply ridged, monster-sized leaves of the giant rhubarb (*Gunnera manicata*) add a steamy, tropical feel to this Zone 6 garden.

While at home in the Southwest, the highly textural prickly pear (*Opuntia gosseliniana* 'Santa Rita') and yucca (*Yucca filamentosa*) can also thrive in Zones 5-10.

To re-create this same effect in a garden far from the tropics, consider using cold-hardy plants with similar textures. Plants such as Japanese aralia (*Aralia elata* 'Silver Umbrella', USDA Zones 4–9), Tiger Eyes staghorn sumac (*Rhus typhina* 'Bailtiger', Zones 4–8) or sweet coltsfoot (*Petasites japonicus*, Zones 4–8) will easily give your garden a tropical atmosphere.

On the other hand, perhaps you're longing for a cottage-style garden similar to the ones you visited in England? Fine-textured plants with delicate foliage and flowers are key elements in that garden style. Examples might include perennials such as grasses, cottage pinks, delphiniums or spirea.

If the rolling hills of a prairie or the natural look of a meadow are what you'd like to see in your garden, include plenty of plants with low-growing, wispy, strap-like foliage. Examples to include would be grasses, perennials, such as Shasta daisy (*Leucanthemum × superbum*), coreopsis (*Coreopsis lanceolata*) or aster, and bulbs that naturalize, such as fritillaria, Narcissus, freesia and crocus.

Many who garden in colder, dry climates long for the look of a warm, Southwestern garden, overflowing with highly structural, bumpy, spiky and thorny textured plants. It's true that below-freezing temperatures and consistently wet roots are less than desirable (if not fatal) to most Southwestern plants, but there are plenty of exceptions. Gardens in Zone 5 climates can successfully grow many varieties of yuccas (*Yucca filamentosa, Y. glauca*), agaves (*Agave parryi, A. utahensis*), chollas (*Cylindropuntia whipplei, C. spinosior*) and prickly pears (*Opuntia humifusa, O. macrocentra*), to name a few. Combine these with other plants with similarly textured foliage, such as globe thistles (*Echinops* spp.), sea hollies (*Eryngium planum*) and the wingthorn rose (*Rosa sericea*), to continue the Southwestern feel in a colder-climate garden.

CHANGE YOUR GARDEN'S PERSONALITY

If your garden isn't a reflection of who you are, perhaps it's time you both take a personality test. Generally, personal gardens are most enjoyable when they're truly a reflection of their creators. When the gardener and garden are out of sync, the result can be a little jarring to both visitors and the homeowner. While there's no right or wrong style of garden, at the end of the day, it should be a place that provides you with inspiration, peace, comfort and happiness.

If that's not what you're experiencing, perhaps its time to rethink the mood and personality of your garden to see if it's in line with yours. If you find your garden is mismatched with your personality, oftentimes adding or eliminating basic elements, such as texture, can easily help remedy the situation.

Casual, Warm and Inviting

When thinking of a grandmother's welcoming lap, a down-filled chair or your favorite chenille sweater, softness is an adjective that most likely comes to mind. Foliage and flowers with textures such as *fuzzy*, *velvety*, *frilly*, *lacy*, *frothy* and *airy* are welcome in any warm and inviting garden. Just imagine a cozy English garden, overflowing with a jumble of delicate and cheery textures. Examples might include: lambs' ear (*Stachys byzantina*), Artemisia, coral bells (*Heuchera* spp.), lady's mantle (*Alchemilla mollis*), lavender and cosmos.

Formal, Proper and Serious

Uniformity, restraint, structure and consistency are key elements found in formal gardens, similar to the established gardens of grand estates. No flamboyant surprises here! But small, fine and consistently textured foliage and flowers are welcome. Examples might include: the needle-like foliage of yew (*Taxus baccata*), the uniformly jagged foliage of boxleaf euonymus (*Euonymus japonicus* 'Microphyllus') and the small and smooth foliage of boxwood (*Buxus* spp.).

Edgy, Contemporary and Cutting Edge

The words *cutting edge* are a clear indication of characteristics that tend to fall within contemporary gardens. Many times this style of garden is filled with angular, geometric and spherical shapes to create a streamlined and highly

Uniformity in color and texture help create a formal and distinguished atmosphere.

Colorful flowers with lacy, frilly and delicate foliage epitomize a casual, warm and welcoming garden.

structured atmosphere. Textures that fit within this category need to coordinate with the angles and structured simplicity of this garden, such as sleek, shiny, polished or sharp. Examples might include the shiny spears of astelias (*Astelia chathamica* 'Silver Shadow'), the sleek and slender foliage of bamboo (*Bambusa* spp.) or the tight, nubby globes of allium and *Echinop* flowers.

Playful, Carefree and Childlike

Carefree and inquisitive children love nothing more than to explore the tiniest details of a garden. Put yourself in a child's shoes to help remind you of the magical and irresistible desire to explore. A playful garden has a mix of textures that are begging to be touched, with flowers and foliage that are fuzzy, furry, spiky, sticky, shiny, crinkly, bristly and feathery. Specific examples might include the fuzzy bunny tails of the Red Bunny Tails grass (*Pennisetum messiacum*), the translucent silver "coins" of the money plant (*Lunaria annua*) or the chenille-like flowers of a love-lies-bleeding (*Amaranthus caudatus*).

Dramatic, Over-the-Top and Flamboyant

Extreme personalities call for extreme textures—no shy wallflowers here! Take an ordinary texture and amplify it to outrageous proportions and you have the perfect drama queen to flounce around the garden.

The oversized, polished leaves of a banana plant (*Ensete* spp.), the steely, prickly flowers of the sea holly (*Eryngium zabelii*), the silvery thread-like filaments that delicately dangles from the *Yucca filamentosa*, and the attention-grabbing, polished, polka-dotted foliage of the leopard plant (*Farfugium japonicum* 'Aureomaculatum') all add theatrical drama to the garden.

Mellow, Easy-Going and Relaxed

Calm as a stroll on an early misty morning, textures that are wispy, needle-like, velvety and silky help create a soothing and relaxed atmosphere in a garden.

Consider the velvety petals of a petunia or cosmos flower, the cloud-like effect of fennel's light and airy textures, or the delicate lacework of an elderberry (*Sambucus nigra* 'Eva' Black Lace).

It's all about geometric shapes in this contemporary garden, filled with spiky and bristly foliage and flowers.

Who could resist the impulse to pet the foliage of the silver sage (*Salvia argentea*)?

ADD MOTION TO YOUR GARDEN

Who doesn't appreciate an unexpected refreshing summer breeze on a sweltering hot summer day? Or the sound of the wind as it rustles through the blades of an ornamental grass? Besides the very real, tangible effects of motion in the garden, the illusion of motion is just as powerful.

Adding the *perception* of motion introduces a subtle (yet no less important) interactive and dynamic element to the garden. For example, despite the weather, the thin and wispy foliage and flowers of many plants will give the illusion of swaying in the wind, moving through the garden or cascading downward like a waterfall.

In addition to strappy, wispy foliage, don't forget the effects that drifts of small, delicate flowers can have in a garden. When woven throughout, these airy flowers appear to float from bed to bed and keep the eye dancing as they subtly lead one through the garden.

Feverfew's light and airy flowers (*Tanacetum parthenium*) appear to float through the landscape, carrying the eye along with them.

CHANGE YOUR GARDEN'S VISUAL BALANCE

As discussed in chapter two, a garden that looks out of balance can create an uneasy feeling. Factors such as inconsistent garden bed dimensions, oppressive and overgrown plants or the ill-chosen use of certain colors and textures can all contribute to this unfortunate end result. Luckily, in addition to color, plants with certain textures can also appear to have visual weight, seeming lighter or heavier than their surrounding neighbors. This is an important illusion when restoring balance to a garden.

Generally speaking, high-contrast textures (i.e., rough, bristly, thick or leathery) on a small plant can easily seem just as heavy as a much larger plant with low-contrast textures (i.e., polished, smooth and matte). Rough textures can also contain ridges with various degrees of depth, resulting in minute shadows that produce a captivating three-dimensional effect. The eye perceives these slightly shadowy, high-contrast textures as having much more visual weight than plants with flat, smooth or matte textures.

The illusion of visual weight is crucial when resetting the scales in an unbalanced garden bed. For example, if your garden bed contains an oversized and imposing shrub, the first thought might be to use another plant of equal size to counterbalance its visual weight. However, it may be more effective (not to mention more interesting) to use a smaller plant with highly textured foliage to bring the scales back to center.

While a highly textured plant can create balance, drifts of delicate textures can also be used for the same effect. For example, the mass created by a band of delicate, cloud-like Arkansas bluestar (Amsonia hubrichtii) or the wispy, arching blades of dwarf mondo grass (Ophiopogon japonicus 'Nana') or even a traditional lawn can all be used as a soothing, yet visually heavy, counterbalance to a substantially sized plant.

Don't you want to run down this pathway with your hands outstretched, brushing against the chenille-like pendants of the grass?

Even without a hint of a breeze, goat's beard (*Aruncus dioicus*) flowers appear to gently wave in the wind.

Though small in comparison to the towering Japanese maple, the bold, tight balls of the peony flowers counterbalance the nearby fine and delicate textures, providing visual balance in this garden bed.

The cascading hakone grass (*Hakonechloa macra* 'Aureola') has the intensity of a crashing wave in the garden.

This garden is a textural delight, with dramatic combinations of furry, bristly, shiny, strappy, crinkly and polished foliage. It was designed by Freeland and Sabrina Tanner of Proscape Landscape Design.

TEXTURE ECHOES:
TAKING IT UP A NOTCH

The clever use of texture can be a practical workhorse in the garden, and when echoed throughout the landscape, is one more way to weave another layer of unity throughout your garden. With unity, comes harmony. Though textural layers may sometimes be subtle they're, nonetheless, powerful. Some of the most harmonious gardens have many subtle layers that come together as a whole to create an unforgettable experience.

A simple way to begin introducing texture echoes into your garden is to experiment with the foliage of different plants to discover, and then repeat, their similar textural qualities. For example, combine the round, polished leaves of a mirror plant (*Coprosma repens*) with a nearby *Hebe* 'Amy', or the lacy foliage of Artemisia with that of an astilbe.

Once you feel comfortable with creating texture echoes with foliage, graduate to another level of complexity by creating echoes between the flowers and foliage of different plants. For example, pair the fuzzy, nubby texture of foxglove leaves (*Digitalis purpurea*) with equally fuzzy flowers of pink mulla mulla (*Ptilotus exaltatus* 'Joey'). The ruffled leaves of coral bells (*Heuchera* spp.) pair beautifully with the ruffled flowers of many azaleas. While the two plants are distinctly different, their subtle texture is the commonality that links the two.

After experimenting with color echoes (discussed in chapter two) and now texture echoes, you'll discover your garden soon begins to have a "wow factor" effect on all who visit. It's subtle, yet powerful, layers such as these that will help transform your weary garden into an unforgettable oasis.

The grass's slender, wispy textures are echoed in the nearby cuphea flowers, resulting in an airy and light combination.

The smooth and silky lily-pad leaves of the nasturtium are echoed by the viola's equally smooth flowers.

LOOKING BEYOND THE LEAF

As you gain more confidence creating texture echoes between foliage and flowers, you'll most likely begin to notice many other sources of texture provided by plants: things like seedpods, old growth, stems and bark. By seeking out the less obvious aspects of plants, you can then create complex texture echoes. Many of these complex echoes are subtle, but their influence on the garden's overall harmony is strong. Since many unusual sources of texture are seasonal, these transitory complex echoes will help carry your garden's design throughout the year, resulting in dynamic, year-round interest.

BARK

Texture is a vital element in the winter landscape, taking center stage when there is little else in the garden provid-

ing visual interest. This is especially true in cold climates with heavy snowfall. Tree bark is a crucial source of texture, providing drastic contrast (and visual relief) against the seemingly endless sea of snow.

But let's not forget the other seasons of the year and the trees whose bark shines brightest. For example, the bark of the crape myrtle (*Lagerstroemia indica*) has a smooth patchwork of muted, earth-toned colors that appear in early spring. The exfoliating and shaggy bark of the strawberry tree (*Arbutus menziesii*) reveals itself in the summer, tempting children to try to resist pulling it off in long strips. The peeling, cinnamon-colored bark of the paperbark maple (*Acer griseum*) is a sight to behold in the garden, rivaling the attention of any nearby fall foliage.

The curling strips of the paperbark maple are a spectacle to behold in the fall garden.

The firework display of allium seedpods add a festive note to the late summer garden.

The feather-duster seed heads of the clematis vine are a show in and of themselves.

SEEDPODS

Even though many texture echoes are seasonal, lasting just a few weeks or so, they're a golden opportunity to create year-round interest, nonetheless. Don't forget that gardens are forever changing, with different layers shining brightest at different times of the year. It's these moments of fleeting beauty, occurring throughout the four seasons of the year, that make a garden truly spectacular.

Seedpods of spent flowers are an excellent source of seasonal interest, providing many opportunities to create complex texture echoes. For example, consider planting a clematis, with its wispy seed heads, near a silver birch (*Betula utilis* var. *jacquemontii*), with its bright, papery peeling bark, to make a textural impact in the fall. Or create an explosive combination by combining the starlike seedpods of an ornamental onion (*Allium christophii*) with a goldenrod's (*Solidago rugosa* 'Fireworks') yellow, arching firework-flowers.

NEW GROWTH

The new growth of many plants also exhibits unusual textures and provides yet another opportunity for complex textural echoes in the garden. Fern fronds often emerge resembling furry sea creatures, and when paired next to a similarly shaggy plant (such as a redwood, cedar or strawberry tree), create quite a textural surprise. Other plants with textural new growth include the golden elderberry (*Sambucus racemosa* 'Sutherland Gold') with its finely serrated, pink

Fern fronds, resembling furry sea creatures, are especially textural when first emerging in the spring.

and ultrapolished new growth, or the tight, silky clusters of emerging pasque flowers (*Pulsatilla hirsutissima*) as they push through the last remains of winter's snow.

EDIBLES

Not only is it more common to combine edibles and ornamentals in the same garden bed, it's almost a shame not to! Integrating edibles throughout the garden makes perfect sense as a way to take advantage of the sunnier areas, to add seasonal spots of color, and to create complex texture echoes.

For example, pairing the bold and deeply ridged leaves of a hosta (Hosta 'Paradigm') with the equally bold and crinkly leaves of a Tuscan kale (or 'Lacinato' kale) is a match made in textural heaven. Other examples of touchable edibles are the fuzzy leaves of garden sage (Salvia officinalis), the fine and wispy foliage of dill, fennel (Foeniculum vulgare) or anise (Pimpinella anisum), the fluffy, curly foliage of parsley and the bristly, prickly leaves of a borage plant.

The contrasting textures of the columbine and stone wall cause the eye to stop and take notice of this unique combination.

NON-LIVING SOURCES OF TEXTURE

As previously discussed in chapter two, there's so much more to your garden than plants and trees. Nonliving elements such as hardscaping (patios, pathways, fences and stones), containers, structures and even artwork can all provide a foundation of year-round texture from which to create another complex echo. While these elements might recede into the background when the plants take center stage, in a garden's quiet months, it's the nonliving textures that carry your garden through winter's bleakest days.

HARDSCAPING MATERIALS

Materials such as concrete, brick, wood, stone, steel and glass offer endless opportunities to create complex texture echoes in the garden. Whether repeating or contrasting these textures with nearby plants, the natural elements from which many of these hardscaping materials are made should be viewed as another textural tool in your design arsenal.

For example, consider pairing the rough and chunky texture of stone columns or a chipped limestone wall with the similarly textured foliage of hydrangeas, mahonias, sumac or viburnums. On the other hand, smooth surfaces, such as polished flagstone, marble, granite or steel, pair exceptionally well with the small and delicate foliage of lavender, spirea, coreopsis and many types of ferns, creating a complex texture echo that contributes to a light and airy atmosphere.

But remember, *harmony* shouldn't mean *monotony*! As in many things in life, if a little is good, a lot isn't necessarily better. Too much repetition can have an adverse effect in the garden, lulling the poor visitor to sleep with one repetitive echo after another.

It's critical to remember the importance of introducing areas of contrast in the garden, in addition to repetition, as a way to add a much-needed jolt of excitement. The textures of hardscaping are an ideal element for adding the perfect amount of subtle contrast. For example, planting a delicate and airy columbine (with its see-through qualities) in front of a rough stone wall is a subtle way to emphasize both textures.

Top left: The layered, papery texture of the flower bracts of the ornamental oregano (*Origanum libanoticum*) is subtly repeated in the layered appearance of the nearby stone.

Top middle: Both the gray color and the smooth, polished texture of the succulent (*Echeveria* spp.) are echoed in the nearby river stones.

Top right: The coarse and chunky limestone wall contrasts nicely with the delicate tracery of the clematis vine.

Middle left: The narrow, elongated foliage of the bamboo are repeated with the thin and narrow reed fencing.

Bottom left: The rusty red colors of the aloes and bricks, combined with the rough and bumpy textures of both, create a complex color and texture echo.

DESIGN TIP

Who says containers must always be planted? Unplanted containers not only provide a welcome contrast to a planting bed, but they're another opportunity to introduce a texture echo. Try pairing the rough and bumpy surface of a concrete urn or the smooth, polished ceramic pot with nearby foliage of similar textures.

CONTAINERS AND ART

Containers and artwork are more than pretty embellishments in your garden; they're also ways to introduce complex echoes into the landscape. For example, consider repeating the slick texture of a galvanized steel container with the equally smooth foliage of camellias, hollies or ginger lilies.

On the other hand, if your garden is in need of a little excitement, don't forget to include contrasting textures. For example, pair a smooth ceramic pot with bristly plants, such as a sea holly or dwarf bottlebrush.

STRUCTURES

Last, but not least, consider the texture of structures within your garden, such as rustic potting sheds and garden nooks or reflective glass greenhouses. Adding this final layer to your complex texture echoes will elevate your garden to new heights, creating a subtle, yet unforgettable, experience.

Top: The rough texture of the concrete St. Francis statue is further echoed by the dramatic and highly textural knife leaf acacia.

Middle: The terra-cotta pot and *Oxalis* 'Sunset Velvet' create a harmonious combination of color and texture.

Bottom: The bold and deeply serrated foliage of the *Fatsia japonica* stands up to the highly textural garden structure, helping them both blend in with the surrounding garden.

Opposite page: The sophisticated combination of burgundy color echoes combined with contrasting textures of the chunky stone column, rough cement finial and smooth foliage create a dynamic, yet serene, composition.

A LESSON IN CONTRAST AND REPETITION

DESIGN SPOTLIGHT

Not only is the burgundy color echoed throughout this garden bed, but textures are as well. Flowers, foliage and nearby hardscaping provide textural echoes, as well as much-needed contrast, combining in such a way as to create a visually rich display.

1. The frilly, ruffled textures of the rhododendron flowers (*Rhododendron* 'Red Eye' and *R.* 'Daphnoides') are echoed in the foliage of the two heucheras (*H.* 'Plum Pudding' and *H.* 'Amethyst Myst').

2. Fine and delicate textures are provided by the needle-like foliage of cold-hardy sedum (*Sedium rupestre* 'Angelina') and the lacy foliage of the Japanese maple (*Acer palmatum* 'Inaba Shidare').

3. Contrasting delicate and bold textures are combined in a 2:1 ratio, allowing enough contrast to provide visual interest while still remaining harmonious.

4. Additional textures are provided by the shiny, hard and rough stones surrounding the garden bed.

CHAPTER 4

FORM

Form, shape and line are to good garden design what proper layout, structure and composition are to an inviting and functional home. The elements in the garden (living and man-made) perform similar functions as the elements in the home: dividing large spaces, creating intimate areas, providing focal points, or leading and engaging the visitor.

The garden of Freeland and Sabrina Tanner demonstrates the refreshing harmony that can be achieved through the skillful combination of forms and shapes.

REMEMBER GEOMETRY?

At its core, a desirable home is built with a strong framework consisting of (among other things) strategically placed walls, counters, kitchen islands, soaring ceilings, pass-through windows, etc., all carefully thought through to help define its overall flow and atmosphere. Whether open and airy, intimate and cozy or a combination of both, the careful placement of these functional elements is what helps set the stage of a home's functionality and visual harmony.

Memorable and functional gardens are no different, with the framework consisting of pathways, fences, arbors, garden rooms and focal points all serving the same functions as those of a well built home. As this book primarily focuses on plants and ways to use them to refresh your garden, the focus of this chapter will be how to harness the power of a particular plant's form, shape and line.

As a landscape designer, I've noticed time and again that the concepts of using *shape*, *form* and *line* in the garden are some of the most challenging for many gardeners to grasp fully. The main reason for the confusion is the similarity of their definitions. As subtle as the differences may be, each element is distinctly different and, once understood, can be used to serve various functions in the garden.

WHAT IS SHAPE?

When discussing a plant's different elements, its shape refers to its *two-dimensional* qualities, otherwise known as the outline, silhouette or contour.

When looking at a plant head-on, imagine drawing a line around the general structure of the plant. That line would be considered its shape. Examples of different plant shapes might include a fountain (e.g. *Spiraea prunifolia* or bridal wreath spirea), a vase (e.g., *Hamamelis* or witch hazel), a column (e.g., *Ginkgo biloba* 'Princeton Sentry') or a sphere (e.g., *Pittosporum tenuifolium* 'Golf Ball').

This spirea is an excellent example of a fountain shape in the garden.

The colorful and deeply lobed leaves of an oakleaf hydrangea (*Hydrangea quercifolia*) are an eye-catching shape to add to the garden.

When looking at a plant's finer details, shape typically refers to the outline of its leaves; heart-shaped, triangular, round, or deeply lobed are just a few descriptions. As discussed in chapters two and three, the color and texture of foliage are powerful characteristics, but as you'll discover in this chapter, the shape of a leaf is also a force to contend with.

WHAT IS FORM?

The form of a plant is *three-dimensional* and includes depth along with the outline or contour. Another way to define form is the overall shape of a plant *when in leaf* (the leaves emphasize the depth). On the other hand, when plants are dormant (without leaves), it's their shapes (or two-dimensional outlines) that are most noticeable in the garden.

The *depth* of a plant is the key factor when discussing form, providing a plant with visual weight, movement and dimension. Examples of form include the spreading dwarf balsam fir (*Abies balsamea* 'Hudsonia'), the conical dwarf Alberta spruce (*Picea glauca* 'Conica') or the twisting dwarf black locust (*Robinia pseudoacacia* 'Lace Lady' Twisty Baby).

WHAT IS LINE?

In garden design, line often refers to the various *visual directions* created by the lines of various elements, such as pathways or focal points. But line also refers to the visual directions and silhouettes of plants. Examples of visual directions a plant might have include the diagonal lines of flax (*Phormium* spp.), the vertical lines of feather reed grass (*Calamagrostis* × *acutiflora* 'Karl Foerster') or the curved lines of the octopus agave (*Agave vilmoriniana* 'Variegata'). A plant's line serves many of the same functions as those of hardscaping elements; they lead the eye to a particular area (lines going away from you), slow the eye down (horizontal lines) or create a sense of mystery (curving lines) or movement (vertical lines).

The American arborvitae (*Thuja occidentalis*) naturally grows in a conical form.

The strong, diagonal lines of the flax (*Phormium* spp.) help to create dynamic energy and a sense of movement in the garden.

HOW TO USE FORM IN THE GARDEN

In a beautiful piece of music, harmony results from the creative combination of various instrumental sounds. The same can be said for creating harmony in the garden, though the instruments of choice here are the various forms and shapes provided by plants.

An understanding of the various functions provided by a plant's form and shape is the first step in identifying which plant to use and where.

BONES OF THE GARDEN

A garden with good form, shape and line is often referred to as a garden with "good bones." Similar to the strength and support provided by the bones in our bodies, a garden's bones provide a year-round solid and sturdy framework for the entire garden.

In addition to a garden's colorful flowers (ephemeral beauty that comes and goes with seasonal changes), a framework of dependable plants with solid structure is at the heart

The bones of the garden continue to carry the garden through the winter months, when many plants are dormant.

The framework of boxwood, structures and vertical evergreen shrubs contains the enthusiasm of this emerging spring garden.

of every successful border. Strong form prevents a garden from going down with a whimper in the blistering hot days of August, when many flowering perennials have grown weary. When placed in the middle and at both ends of a bed, reliable plants with strong form act as anchors, ensuring the garden has interest, beauty and stability every day of the year. Without this form, a free-flowing garden bed can quickly transform into a jumbled and listless mess appearing to have no rhyme or reason.

Unfortunately, this is a common scenario with beginning gardeners, as their focus isn't on long-term, year-round interest but instead on the here-and-now gratification provided by the colorful and overflowing nursery aisles. New gardeners may be thrilled with their beds in May and June when every plant is in full bloom, then quickly become frustrated and disappointed with their garden's performance the rest of the year. More often than not, the cause of their dismay is the garden's lack of form.

DESIGN TIP

Consider winter the perfect opportunity to review your sleeping garden's framework. Note any areas of
missing form by comparing your dormant winter garden with garden photos you've taken throughout the year.
Visit local botanical gardens to note winter plants that stand out with impressive shapes and lines.

Evergreen shrubs and trees (such as dwarf conifers, yew or boxwood) are usually the first plants that come to mind when referring to the bones of a garden as they offer their solid reassurance every day of the year. Anchoring an over-abundant perennial bed in the spring and summer, they also provide year-round interest in the waning days of fall and faithful support throughout the bleak days of winter. However, in addition to evergreens, don't forget the stunning and valuable framework provided by deciduous plants as well.

WINTER INTEREST

If your garden's colorful tapestry seems a little threadbare in the winter, perhaps it needs an injection of form, shape and line. Evergreen plants that have a substantial form, such as

The unique umbrella shape of the weeping mulberry shines brightest in the winter once every last leaf has dropped.

When in full leaf, the draping form of the weeping mulberry tree (*Morus alba* 'Pendula') is a delightful surprise to find in the garden.

arborvitae (*Thuja occidentalis* 'Degroot's Spire') or holly (*Ilex glabra* 'Compacta'), have the strength and volume to stand up to oppressive mounds of snow and still provide attractive shapes in the garden.

Many deciduous plants also have the necessary shapes and lines to provide a garden with winter structure. During the winter months, when their leaves are long gone, the lines of many dormant plants take center stage, with some, in fact, actually looking their best. Winter allows many plants with extreme shapes to show off their normally hidden lines, such as the twisting branches of Harry Lauder's walking stick (*Corylus avellana* 'Contorta'), the weeping lines of a Euorope-an white birch (*Betula pendula*) and the dramatic shape of a weeping mulberry (*Morus alba* 'Pendula').

LIVING SCREENS

Everyone wants a little privacy in their gardens, but with the trend these days of larger homes with smaller gardens, finding that privacy is becoming quite a challenge. A typical solid fence may offer the most privacy from prying eyes, but it's not always the ideal solution. One reason is that most cities have municipal codes that restrict the height of a fence. Plants, on the other hand, are allowed to grow much taller and can, therefore, provide more privacy. Another reason gardeners may not want a fence surrounding their property is the somewhat uninviting atmosphere (i.e., stay out!) a solid fence can create. And let's not forget the upkeep a fence requires (including re-staining and replacing rotted wood) and the lifespan of the fence (typically one or two decades at most).

Quite often, carefully chosen trees can be ideal screening solutions. As they can grow much taller, they're more inviting to look at and their longevity outlasts most wooden fences. The form and shape of a plant are two critical factors to consider when using them for privacy. For example, in smaller spaces look for vertical, columnar or cone shapes—those that grow taller than they grow wide. Plants that naturally grow with these tidy, narrow forms can be planted closer to the property line without actually infringing on your neighbor's property. Examples include the Norway spruce (*Picea abies* 'Cupressina'), boxleaf azara (*Azara microphylla*) and compact cherry laurel (*Prunus caroliniana* 'Bright 'N Tight').

The evergreen "living fence" in this front yard provides year-round screening and privacy between two neighbors far beyond what the height of a traditional fence could offer.

The smaller size of the crape myrtle (*Lagerstroemia indica* 'Dynamite') continues to provide more privacy than the fence, but it offers summer flowers and fall color as well.

In addition to trees, smaller growing shrubs are also an excellent choice for privacy as they are less likely to overwhelm a smaller garden. Even though most shrubs will never reach towering heights, they can still be easily trained into small trees that may be more appropriate for tighter spaces. Examples include evergreen Carolina cherry laurel (*Prunus caroliniana*), hopseed bush (*Dodonaea viscosa* 'Purpurea') and kohuhu (*Pittosporum tenuifolium*).

The next point to consider is whether or not year-round screening is desired. If so, plants that keep their leaves year-round (evergreen) are your best options, including varieties such as arborvitae (*Thuja occidentalis* 'Emerald'), English yew (*Taxus baccata*) or Skyrocket juniper (*Juniperus scopulorum* 'Skyrocket'). Keep in mind that while evergreen plants provide year-round screening, that's just about all they provide. They're less likely to be focal points or accents in the garden, acting more like wallpaper that remains quietly in the background.

On the other hand, don't be too quick to rule out deciduous plants as screening options. True, the missing leaves mean less privacy in the winter, but the trade-off is more winter sunlight that will filter through your garden. Deciduous plants also offer other elements for year-round interest, such as brilliant fall foliage, textural tree bark, colorful berries and attractive winter shapes and lines. Examples include hornbeam (*Carpinus betulus* 'Frans Fontaine'), silver birch (*Betula utilis* var. *jacquemontii*) and the coral bark maple (*Acer palmatum* 'Sango-kaku').

LIVING STRUCTURES

The different forms and shapes of plants can also be creatively used to perform the functions of living structures in the garden. Many typical structures (such as arbors, plant supports or archways) are made of rigid wood or metal and are, therefore, angular in shape. However, curving and softer shapes are possible when using shrubs that are long, narrow and pliable.

DESIGN TIP

Did you know that strategically placed deciduous trees and shrubs have the potential to also reduce your electricity bills? When placed at the southwest corner of the house, a deciduous tree will allow for maximum winter warmth from the sun's rays. And during the hottest days of summer, when the tree is in full leaf, the tree will provide your home with much needed shade!

The columnar shape of the hornbeam (*Carpinus betulus*) offers privacy and shade in the summer months. After the plant goes dormant, winter's warm sunlight can gently filter through the garden.

A welcoming, casual and rustic archway is created by training two narrow cypress trees to grow together.

Too much repetition can quickly turn harmony into monotony

CREATE VARIETY

It's true what they say: Variety is the spice of life. As in most parts of life, if everything remains the same it soon becomes a bit boring. Gardens are no different. While repetition throughout a garden's different layers (i.e., color, texture, form and shape) creates a sense of unity and rhythm, too much repetition can quickly turn harmony into monotony.

If your garden has more predictability than pizzazz, the solution might be as straightforward as injecting it with a healthy dose of contrast. Contrast creates dynamic energy through the visual tension created by different elements (e.g., complementary or opposing colors textures or shapes).

PROVIDE CONTRAST

As mentioned previously in this book, your camera is one of the most powerful tools in your design tool bag, helping to diagnose many different problem areas in your garden. Take it one step further by stripping away the color; a black-and-white photo can also help pinpoint the contrast (or lack thereof) of light, color, shape and form in a garden bed. Getting the ratio of contrast to repetition just right can sometimes be tricky to master. Too much repetition of similar forms and the plants will blend together into a giant, uninteresting mass; too much contrast among shapes, with no areas of visual rest, and the garden will appear overly chaotic.

DESIGN TIP

When introducing a plant with a strong form, it's important to keep its impact strong by surrounding the plant with lower-growing plants that won't compete for your attention.

This garden bed would still look stunning without the Sky Pencil holly (*Ilex crenata* 'Sky Pencil'), but its strong form adds a surprising jolt of excitement.

Opposite page, top: This dynamic combination looks good both in color and black and white. The dramatic and upright form of the Cape rush (*Chondropetalum tectorum*) contributes to the pleasing visual tension.

Opposite page, middle: Once the color is removed, it's evident that there's too much repetition in this garden, from both the shape of the foliage and the form of the plants. Introducing a stronger form would help wake things up.

Opposite page, bottom: The frothy gray santolina (*Santolina chamaecyparissus*) provides a billowy contrast between the spiky forms of both the fortnight lily (*Dietes iridioides*) and the cordyline.

WAKE A SLEEPY GARDEN

To prevent a garden from lulling one to sleep through its excessive use of gentle mounding shapes, vertical plant forms are needed to act as your garden's midday shot of caffeine. Like exploding rockets, vertical plants are guaranteed to keep a garden lively.

Shrubs and trees with columnar forms, such as Lombardy poplar (*Populus nigra* 'Italica'), columnar boxwood (*Buxus sempervirens* 'Graham Blandy') or Italian cypress (*Cupressus sempervirens*), act as solitary exclamation points in your garden's otherwise quiet conversation. Using a grouping of vertical shapes in the garden can soften the impact of using a solitary specimen. However, just like in pleasant conversation, it's necessary to use restraint (just imagine talking to someone who only uses exclamation points!!).

For a smaller jolt of electricity, incorporate the vertical shapes provided by many flowers, grasses and succulents into your garden beds. Instead of using them as solitary specimens, maximize the impact of their smaller size by planting them in groups or drifts. Examples include spiked speedwell (*Veronica spicata*), blazing stars (*Liatris* cvs.), lupines (*Lupinus* cvs.) and feather reed grass (*Calamagrostis* × *acutiflora* 'Karl Foerster').

COMMAND ATTENTION

Plants with strong forms or shapes also serve as focal points in the garden and, when used strategically, can solve a wide range of everyday garden problems. One of the most noteworthy roles of a focal point is to control the line of sight, helping to lead the eye to a specific destination in the garden. That destination may be a visual one (emphasizing a spectacular view, for example) or it may be a literal destination (beckoning visitors to explore a certain part of the garden).

But a focal point plant can also lead the eye *away* from a view, as well, which is especially helpful when that view is less than desirable (e.g., a neighboring roofline, unsightly utility pole or air-conditioning unit). The first inclination may be to plant the focal point directly in front of the eyesore in an attempt to block it entirely from view. Unfortunately, this strategy can quickly backfire and have the opposite effect by acting as a spotlight on the very thing it's trying to hide.

Instead, place the focal point plant slightly *away* from the offending object. Plant less attention-grabbing plants (those with softer shapes, colors and textures) in front of the eyesore to help obscure it from view, and use the focal point's strong form and shape to redirect the attention onto a more desirable area of the garden. The ideal focal point plants in the garden aren't necessarily the ones with the most dramatic forms or shapes; they just need to stand apart from their surroundings in order to grab one's attention.

For maximum impact, it's essential to use restraint when placing focal point plants in the garden, as the goal is for the eye to focus on a single element or grouping. If too many focal points are planted in one area, the result will be a chaotic grouping with each plant competing with its neighbor, loudly crying out for one's attention.

EMPHASIZE A GARDEN'S SKYLINE

A garden's skyline is much like that of a city, but instead of the horizon being composed of the silhouettes of buildings, it's created by the outlines of plants. For those gardeners lucky enough to be surrounded by nature, the outline of their garden can often be used to highlight the naturally occurring lines of their setting. For example, if rolling hillsides surround the garden, use similarly shaped mounding plants to create a *line echo*.

On the other hand, if the space seems too large with a seemingly endless horizon, you may wish to create a "hard stop" to signify the end of the garden. Using plants on your garden's horizon, with forms that contrast with their natural surroundings, will help bring the space down in scale, and create a more intimate atmosphere.

Top left: The gentle forms of mounding geraniums, the fountain-shaped lilies and the tiered, horizontal viburnum are woken up by the vibrant spikes of variegated iris (*Iris pallida* 'Variegata').

Top right: Even the slender and delicate vertical form of the Spanish foxglove (*Digitalis parviflora*) adds a significant dose of visual energy to this garden.

Bottom left: The garden's soft and mounding plants echo the lines of the nearby mountain range.

Bottom right: The powerful upright form of the Skyrocket juniper (*Juniperus scopulorum* 'Skyrocket') helps to distract one's attention from the nearby A/C unit.

DESIGN SPOTLIGHT

SIMPLE CONTRASTS MAKE ALL THE DIFFERENCE

Before Sometimes a few simple changes are all that's needed to revitalize a humdrum garden bed. The original bed was comprised of a lackluster combination of overgrown plants with very little variation in color, texture, shape or form. While the Skyrocket juniper (*Juniperus scopulorum* 'Skyrocket') serves as the anchor in this jumbled garden bed, it's a shame not to highlight its spectacular color and form.

After This simple, refreshing combination results in variations of form, color and texture, while complementing the existing Skyrocket juniper. Except for the berberis and iris, all of the plants are evergreen in this Zone 9 planting bed, providing year round interest to the garden.

BEFORE

AFTER

1. The blue color of the evergreen Skyrocket juniper's finely cut foliage contrasts nicely with the surrounding burgundy and chartreuse colors.

2. Injecting this combination with a bit of excitement is the contrasting spiky foliage of variegated iris (*Iris pallida* 'Variegata').

3. Barberry (*Berberis thunbergii* 'Concorde') provides more contrast with its dark burgundy color, foliage size and open form. While invasive in many parts of the country, California's lack of summer rainfall keeps it in check.

4. The overgrown rockrose (*Cistus* spp.) is replaced with a mid-sized *Grevillea* 'Superb' to take advantage of its contrasting fountain form, the dramatic shape of its foliage and its bold, colorful flowers.

FORM'S OPTICAL ILLUSIONS

There's something gratifying that comes from transforming a predictable garden into something that borders on magical. This is especially true when the transformation includes using a little sleight of hand. As previously mentioned, there are many optical illusions that can be created through the strategic use of color and texture. The same can be said for the form and shape of a plant, and with a little thoughtful placement, they can work their own magic in your garden.

ADD MOTION

Use the many different forms of a plant to help your garden tell a story. Whether your garden's plotline includes a sudden gust of wind, a surprise sense of falling, or even an occasional explosion, understanding the illusions that many forms create will be instrumental in your storytelling abilities.

Many plants with twisting, curving, wavy and diagonal forms add a visually dynamic sense of movement to the garden. Examples include the twisting form of the Twisty Baby dwarf black locust (*Robinia pseudoacacia* 'Lace Lady' Twisty Baby), the layered lines of many viburnums (*Viburnum plicatum*) and the curlicue branches of the Harry Lauder's walking stick (*Corylus avellana* 'Contorta').

On the other hand, drawing the eye upward using plants with strong vertical forms can create a literal sense of movement, as the viewer scans the horizon then moves his line of sight up and over the vertical plant. Metaphorically speaking, these "rockets" function as exploding punctuations in the garden, lifting the eye toward the sky. Examples include the dwarf cypress (*Cupressus sempervirens* 'Tiny Tower'), Crimson Pointe Flowering Plum (*Prunus* × *cerasifera* 'Cripoizam') and the Sky Pencil holly (*Ilex crenata* 'Sky Pencil').

Spiky shapes serve a similar function as their larger rocket-like cousins, offering less intense high points in the garden. Flowers from perennials and annuals, as well as

The powerful and dramatic form of the weeping Norway spruce (*Picea abies* 'Pendula') is a show-stopper, resembling a gently cascading waterfall.

The spinning pinwheel (*Puya venusta*) combined with the wavy branches of the deciduous beech tree creates a visually dynamic winter combination.

grasses and succulents, can help create this upward motion. Plants in this category include the velvety flowers of a lamb's ear (*Stachys byzantina*), the thin spikes of a blue oat grass (*Helictotrichon sempervirens*) and the brightly colored rockets of many varieties of aloe.

Trailing, draping, and weeping plants pull the eye downward, creating yet another sense of movement in the garden. Just think of the sprawling form of a spreading juniper (*Juniperus horizontalis* 'Blue Chip' or *J. horizontalis* 'Wiltonii'), the waterfall form of a weeping blue atlas cedar (*Cedrus atlantica* 'Glauca Pendula') or a low-growing sedum cascading over a garden wall.

CHANGE YOUR GARDEN'S MOOD

There are two basic categories of form in the garden, each contributing to the overall mood or atmosphere of the space. *Closed forms* are those that are typically neat and tidy with a tendency to grow evenly and retain their shape over a long period of time (either naturally or with periodic pruning). Plants that fall within this category include those with round, conical, clipped, tight and very symmetrical forms. Examples include many dwarf conifers, conical yews and classic boxwood. Plants with closed forms tend to lend an atmosphere of formality to a garden when mixed throughout.

Plants with *open forms*, on the other hand, create a casual feeling in a garden with their characteristic loose and sculptural shapes. Plants with fountain shapes, billowing forms, and layered or twisting branches all fall within this category and can be used to create an air of informality in the garden. Just imagine the undulating plumes of the smoke tree (*Cotinus coggygria* 'Velvet Cloak'), the fountain shapes provided by many grasses (e.g., *Miscanthus sinensis* 'Morning Light' or *Pennisetum setaceum* 'Rubrum') or the open and airy Russian sage (*Perovskia atriplicifolia* 'Filigran').

The spikes of a torch lily (*Kniphofia uvaria*) add just the right amount of vertical pizzazz to wake a sleeping garden.

A perfect blend of open and closed forms create a balanced and serene mood in the garden, providing year-round variety and interest.

CONTROL YOUR GARDEN'S WEIGHT

What do I mean by the *visual weight* of a plant? Don't worry; I'm not suggesting you physically weigh each plant. Rather, this is the heaviness (or lack thereof) of a plant's appearance. Visual weight in the garden is essential as it accomplishes two things; it creates visual balance, and it helps to anchor a space.

As discussed in chapters two and three, color and texture both contribute to a plant's visual weight. The shape of a plant is another element that can create the illusion of heaviness. For example, if a plant has a compact and sturdy shape (e.g., a closed form, such as a triangle or cone), it will appear to have much more visual weight than a shape that is open (e.g., fountain or spikes). In addition to a plant's overall form or shape, the smaller parts of a plant—for example, small, dense shapes (such as a peony bud or allium flower) or an overly complex shape (such as the flower of a zinnia or a thistle)—can appear heavier, as well.

A garden bed filled with an overabundance of open and airy forms can quickly appear jumbled and overly busy due to the lack of contrast between shapes and forms. To restore order among a chaotic bed such as this, a few strategically placed visually heavy plants provide stability among the free-flowing groupings and reign in their overabundant tendencies. These heavier plants are considered the anchors of the garden bed.

On the other hand, if a garden is filled with too many visually heavy plants, it can quickly become an oppressive, austere and uninviting place to visit. The solution can be as easy as incorporating a few visually light plants (i.e., those with open forms). Just as with any other element of a plant, the concept of contrast and repetition with a plant's form is vital for creating a pleasing atmosphere in the garden.

Top: The strong vertical forms of the hornbeam trees are counterbalanced by the visual weight of the smaller, tightly clipped boxwood balls.

Bottom: The visual weight created by the sotol's strong vertical lines are counterbalanced by the small but complex shape and strong color of the soap aloe's flowers.

Opposite page: This garden includes a perfect blend of visually heavy, round shapes of the boxwood and light, airy shapes of the hakone grass and geranium.

DESIGN TIP

In addition to the visual weight created by a plant, the space of an entire area can appear heavy or light. For example, a smaller area in the garden will seem busy (and therefore heavy) when cluttered with many different shapes. On the contrary, a larger area with minimal shapes and plenty of open space will seem lighter. A harmonious garden is a balancing act between the weights of individual plants and the weights of entire areas.

SHAPES AND THEIR WEIGHT

Readjusting your garden's visual weight sometimes is as easy as using the right shape. Whether it's introducing weight through cones or globes, or adding a feeling of lightness with fountains or spikes, the specific shape of a plant can create quite an impact in your garden.

Fountains

These are plants that are narrower at their base, flare outward at the top and then slightly droop, such as flax (*Phormium* spp.), spirea (*Spiraea prunifolia* or bridal wreath) or maiden grass (*Miscanthus sinensis* 'Morning Light'). Plants with these graceful, open shapes tend to have space between the leaves or blades, letting one see what lies beyond. This trait allows this form to appear both heavy and light at the same time. For example, while a towering flax may dominate a garden bed in size and stature, when the eye can see other plants through its bold, strappy foliage, it appears light, as well.

Spikes

Spiky shapes may sometimes be fountain shaped, but their foliage tends to be more upright and stiff. This is often considered a somewhat masculine form and offers a refreshing break from an abundance of billowing perennials. Examples include yuccas (*Yucca glauca*), cordyline (*Cordyline* 'Red Sensation') and iris.

Globes

Natural anchors in the garden, these heavy and closed forms can also help link together more visually dynamic shapes (such as vertical, spiky or fountain-shaped plants). Shrubs include the naturally rounded Golf Ball kohuhu (*Pittosporum tenuifolium* 'Golf Ball'), dwarf globe blue spruce (*Picea pungens* 'Glauca Globosa') or pruned boxwood (*Buxus* spp.). Many flowers with spherical shapes, such as ornamental onions (*Allium* spp.), globe amaranth (*Gomphrena* spp.) or green lavender cotton (*Santolina rosmarinifolia*), can serve the same functions.

Mounds and Domes

Both forms are considered somewhat heavy and closed, though these shapes tend to appear less severe in the garden than tight forms of spheres. When used at the front of a border, naturally mounding plants can soften the harsh lines where hardscaping and landscaping meet. Examples include threadleaf Japanese maple (*Acer palmatum* 'Crimson Queen'), abelia (*Abelia × grandiflora* 'Kaleidoscope') and sedge (*Carex morrowii* 'Ice Dance').

Cones

Whether used as an accent plant, focal point or anchor, this visually heavy form is a bit softer (and less dramatic) than its straight vertical cousins. While using vertical plants in the garden can certainly add life to a garden, these less dramatic forms can be easier for gardeners to implement in their landscape without fear of creating a visually jarring experience. Examples include many natural conical-shaped Alberta spruces (*Picea glauca* 'Haal'), yew (*Taxus cuspidata* 'Pyramidalis') and holly (*Ilex* 'Nellie R. Stevens').

Mats

Whether talking about low-growing perennials and evergreens or larger but horizontal-shaped shrubs, plants with a mat (or spreading) form create the illusion of grounding the garden to its site. Examples include spreading juniper (*Juniperus* 'Icee Blue' or 'Limeglow'), cotoneaster (*Cotoneaster dammeri × suecicus* 'Coral Beauty') and perennials such as lamb's ear (*Stachys byzantina*) or cranesbill geranium (*Geranium × cantabrigiense* 'Biokovo').

THE POWER OF THE TRIANGLE

When it comes to illusions in the garden, triangle shapes reign supreme. Don't worry; I'm not suggesting you shear your shrubs into the formal, clipped triangles of topiary gardens. Instead, I'm referring to the strategic placement of plants within a garden bed to achieve the perception of depth.

Placing plants in a triangular pattern allows the eye to see continuity (i.e., harmony) as well as notice the space between the three plants. This illusion helps to make a small space appear larger.

The strong, conical form of the spruce anchors this primarily perennial garden bed, providing stability throughout the year.

The mid-level weeping European hornbeam (*Carpinus betulus* 'Pendula') forms a spreading mat to ground the surrounding visually light Japanese maples.

The strappy foliage is the common element among these three plants. By placing one along the front of the border and two in the back, an illusion of depth is created.

The three plants share a silver-blue color as well as mounding shapes. When placed within three different tiers of the garden, height and depth is perceived.

The placement of the three gold, mounding abelias (*Abelia ×grandiflora* 'Kaleidoscope') helps guide the visitor through the garden.

To experiment with this concept, it's easiest to use three of the same type of plant, although this effect can certainly be created while using three different plants. The important thing to remember is the three plants in the triangle should share a common element that links them together (e.g., color, texture, shape or form).

In a small garden bed, the tendency is to line similar plants in a straight row. However, placing two plants along the front border and the third in the back (even just a few inches back), creates a perception of depth.

When placing a triangular shape within different tiers (or levels) in the garden, both height and depth is highlighted. For example, place two plants on the lower level and one higher up and the eye begins to sense height as well as depth. The more the eye travels (back and forth, up and down), the greater the illusion of depth.

THE POWER OF THE TRIANGLE

One of geometry's most powerful illusions in the garden is created by the use of triangle shapes. Placing plants with similar traits in a triangular pattern, whether close together or farther apart, creates the illusion of depth. The farther apart each plant in the triangular pattern is, the greater the perceived depth. The plants don't necessarily need to be the same species, but they should share similar characteristics (e.g., color, texture or form). Using different, yet similar, traits not only weaves a harmonious thread throughout your garden's tapestry, but the increased plant palette keeps your garden interesting and diverse.

1. Even though each plant has a different form (e.g., the round pomegranate, the mounding hakone grass and vase-shaped Chinese pistache tree), they share the same vibrant gold colors.

2. Try elevating one of the three plants in the triangle to make the space appear deeper yet, as the eye will not only travel horizontally but vertically, as well.

3. Use fall's fleeting colors as another opportunity to add seasonal harmony in your garden. Though the colors may be temporary, when creatively used, they can make a powerful impact in the garden.

FORM AND SHAPE ECHOES: TAKING IT UP A NOTCH

Armed with an understanding of how a plant's form and shape can be used in the garden, both functionally and to create optical illusions, it's time to tackle the most challenging aspect of this characteristic: the fine art of creating form echoes.

As mentioned in chapters two and three, repeating a plant's particular trait (e.g., color or texture) is often the most effective way to introduce a sense of cohesion throughout the garden. Whether repetition is achieved by using the same plant throughout the garden, or its unique and individual characteristics, one thing is for certain: Layering (or echoing) form throughout the garden is a surefire way to weave cohesion and unity throughout.

Choosing a plant with a unique form and repeating that plant throughout the garden is the simplest, and perhaps most obvious, way to create an echo. For example, repeat the vertical form of a Skyrocket juniper by periodically winding these plants throughout your garden. While there's nothing wrong with this method, why not take it up a notch and introduce *complex form echoes*.

Complex form echoes are created when repeating a plant's form or shape with other, less obvious elements of the garden. For example, instead of repeating the vertical Sky Rocket juniper over and over again in the garden, emphasize its vertical form by repeating it with a flower's vertical shape or a vertical statue.

> **DESIGN TIP**
>
> When creating layers within a garden bed, the rule of thumb is to place low-growing plants in the front, mid-sized plants in the middle and tall plants in the back. To avoid the guaranteed predictability of this strategy, periodically break the rules by planting a taller plant with an open form with see-through qualities in the front. Those see-through qualities prevent the plant from appearing too bulky, while creating a more natural and less-structured garden bed.

Another benefit of complex echoes is that they're often longer-lasting in the garden. While flowers and foliage may come and go throughout the year, the nonliving elements of your garden are year-round and, as such, are the ideal candidates to echo a plant's form.

FORM AND FOLIAGE ECHOES

In addition to creating an echo by repeating the same plant throughout your garden, consider a plant's other characteristics from which to create repetition. Pairing a plant's form with neighboring foliage of similar shapes is one of the easiest ways to create a complex form echo. An added benefit of using foliage to repeat form is its longevity in the garden, lasting several seasons if not year-round.

Examples include pairing a conical-shaped Alberta spruce with the teardrop-shaped foliage of *Houttuynia cordata*, persicaria or camellia. Or consider pairing the vertical form of a 'Princeton Sentry' ginkgo tree with the linear and upright foliage of little bluestem grass (*Andropogon scoparius*), rush (*Juncus patens*) or iris.

A complex form echo is created using the vertical flowers of the Jerusalem sage (*Phlomis russeliana*), the upright fountain and the conical blue spruce in the distance.

FORM AND FLOWER ECHOES

In addition to using foliage to create a complex form echo, consider the many shapes of nearby flowers. Though a bit more fleeting in the garden than foliage, they are nevertheless just as powerful.

Examples include pairing the spherical forms of a dwarf blue spruce (*Picea pungens* 'Glauca Globosa') with the circular-shaped flowers of the globe amaranth (*Gomphrena globosa*), allium, or the dainty flowers of pink knotweed (*Persicaria capitata*). Or you might pair the conical form of a golden hinoki cypress (*Chamaecyparis obtusa* 'Nana Lutea') with the similarly shaped flowers of a coneflower (*Echinacea* spp.), pink mulla mulla (*Ptilotus exaltatus* 'Joey') or pride of Madeira (*Echium* spp.).

The vertical form of the Lawson's false cypress (*Chamaecyparis lawsoniana* 'Ellwoodii') is echoed with the nearby flowers of speedwell (*Veronica spicata* 'Glory') and lamb's ear (*Stachys byzantina*).

The circular shape of nasturtium foliage would be an ideal echo for the round forms of the kohuhu shrub (*Pittosporum tenuifolium* 'Golf Ball').

FORM AND HARDSCAPING ECHOES

As we've learned throughout this book, our gardens consist of so much more than living components. Containers, artwork, fountains, sculptures, gazing globes and even entire garden structures are so much more than pretty accessories in your garden; they're also prime candidates for creating complex echoes.

Unity is achieved when all the different layers of your garden (color, texture, form and shape) share common, yet distinct, characteristics. It's the artful combination (through repetition and contrast) of these different elements that help to transform an ordinary garden into one that's memorable, meaningful and magical.

The shape and color of this garden structure's peaked roofline is echoed with the striking foliage of the artichoke plant.

DESIGN TIP

Winter is the time when the bones of the garden are on display and when your garden's hardscaping will shine brightest. Man-made and man-placed items (walls, fences, arbors, stones, patios, furniture and containers) take center stage during this quiet season, no longer obscured by summer's ever-changing display of color and activity. Year-round seasonal exposure, as well as durability and longevity, is all the more reason to use high-quality materials when introducing these items into your garden.

Conical shapes are echoed in both the tall evergreen and the garden's arbor, adding much-needed structure and interest to this winter garden.

5

PLANT PICKS

The blue-green color, the unique spiral form, and the smooth yet sharp texture of this donkey tail spurge (*Euphorbia myrsinites*) make this a stunning addition to Zone 5-9 gardens.

There's something all gardeners share in common: We love shopping for plants! It's hard to resist finding "one more spot in the garden" for another plant or two. However, I hope you've discovered by now that plants are so much more than decorative elements in your garden; they're practical workhorses as well. In honor of their practicality, superior reliability and jaw-dropping seasonal interest, this chapter is organized by the design solution each plant provides to your garden's overall harmony.

COLOR

COLOR WITH MOVEMENT AND TEMPERATURE

Color is one of the most effective ways to begin refreshing your garden's design, as well as solving a wide range of common everyday garden headaches. One of the most effective uses of color happens also to have a two-for-one punch to it by making a space appear larger (or smaller) than it is while simultaneously appearing warmer or cooler.

VISUALLY WARM AND ACTIVE PLANTS

Papaver dubium
(long-pod poppy)
• USDA Zones—All
• Full sun, moderate water

Persicaria microcephala
'Red Dragon' (knotweed)
• USDA Zones 4–10
• Sun to partial sun, moderate water

Elaeagnus × ebbingei
'Gilt Edge' (silverberry)
• USDA Zones 6–9
• Sun to partial sun, moderate water

One of the truest red flowers to be found, each plant forms a tidy 2' × 2' (0.6m × 0.6m) ferny-leafed mound in the garden, covered with dozens of blooms on long, slender stems. When planted in the distance, the cheerful flowers of this annual act as beacons in the garden, visually jumping forward over their less-colorful neighbors. It's this illusion of movement that causes a smaller space to seem much larger than it is.

A sterile variety of its invasive cousins, this 4' × 4' (1.2m × 1.2m) perennial will stop everyone in their tracks not just once but twice. First, in the spring, the darkly alluring burgundy foliage emerges (with silvery-green accents), commanding all to take notice. Then again in the fall, delicate and airy white blooms cover the contrasting towering stems for weeks at a time.

Quickly growing to 6' × 6' (1.8m × 1.8m) in warm shades of soft gold, this evergreen and thornless shrub is tough as nails, able to withstand heat, drought and frost without showing the slightest hint of irritation. Planted at the back of a semi-shady border or set against a green hedge, silverberry creates quite an impact with its illusion of movement. Happy in sun and shade, this is a very versatile addition to the garden.

VISUALLY COOL AND PASSIVE PLANTS

Cerinthe major
'Purpurascens' (blue honeywort)
• USDA Zones—All
• Partial sun to sun, moderate water

Euphorbia characias
'Glacier Blue' spurge
• USDA Zones 7–9
• Partial sun to sun, low water

Senecio greyi 'Sunshine'
(a.k.a. *Brachyglottis greyi*) (daisy bush)
• USDA Zones 8–10
• Part sun to Sun, Low Water

No other annual causes more excitement in my garden than the yearly show of cerinthe blooms. The nodding, tubular, deep-purple flowers cascade down the blue-gray stems and foliage, resulting in a knockout cool-toned color combination. However, when placed near a warm-colored plant, the illusion of visual movement is nothing less than amazing, working its magic by making a small space feel larger. Hummingbirds and bees love this plant almost as much as I do, and its habit of freely reseeding guarantees I'll have a healthy crop of babies available each spring.

An evergreen perennial growing to a tidy 3' 3' (0.9m 0.9m) mound, 'Glacier Blue' spurge, with its cool blue foliage with creamy margins, appears airy and delicate while visually receding in a small garden bed. One of the few varieties that can thrive in partial shade, its bright colors will add much-needed color to these darker areas of the garden. Its Dr. Seuss-like flowers (creamy white) begin appearing in early spring and last through summer. Its cool colors also visually bring down the temperature on hot days. All parts of the plant contain a milky sap that can be an irritant.

Nothing cools down a hot bed faster than the gray-green velvety foliage of the daisy bush. Each leaf is delicately traced with the thinnest line of white, adding to its cooling qualities. A hardy shrub to include in any sunny border, it requires nothing more than the occasional pinching to keep it bushy and a drink of water when it's hot outside. It has a sporadic burst of yellow daisylike blooms in late summer (though I admit I usually remove them, as I prefer the attention remain on the foliage).

COLOR

COLOR WITH WEIGHT

Certain colors carry more visual weight than others and can be instrumental in correcting a wide range of garden problems. For example, if a garden bed seems disproportional or off balance, a visually heavy plant can tip the scales back to center. Or if a garden seems overly jumbled and chaotic, plants with visual weight can act as anchors. On the other hand, if a garden bed feels dense and oppressive, incorporating lighter colors will lighten the mood, creating an airy atmosphere.

VISUALLY HEAVY PLANTS

Primula vulgaris
'Drumcliff' (primrose)

• USDA Zones 3–10

• Shade to partial sun, moderate water

Carex buchananii 'Red Rooster'
(Buchanan's sedge, leatherleaf sedge)

• USDA Zones 7–10

• Partial sun to sun, moderate to low water

Sambucus nigra
'Eva' Black Lace (elderberry)

• USDA Zones 4–9

• Partial sun to sun, moderate water

Even the smallest of plants can appear to have a hefty dose of visual weight, something that is especially important in the front of the border. When placed up front, their visual weight draws the eye to them first, signaling the brain to "start here" before taking in the rest of the garden bed. This old-fashioned favorite gets a makeover in dusky, dark burgundy foliage that holds its own throughout the season. This cold-hardy primrose is guaranteed to wake your sleeping garden in the early days of spring.

No longer reserved for dead and dormant plants, beautiful shades of bronzy-browns are finding their way into gardens everywhere. The upright form of this 2' × 3' (0.6m × 0.9m) sedge (a grasslike plant in the *Carex* genus) makes it ideal for the front or middle of the border and is especially striking when planted near peach or soft yellow flowers. Prune to the ground in late winter, before new foliage emerges.

Growing quickly to a stately 8' × 8' (2.4m × 2.4m) size, this hardy deciduous shrub is fast becoming a favorite among garden designers. While the inky black color provides visual weight, the delicate, finely cut foliage prevents it from appearing overly cumbersome. Sharing similar traits with many Japanese maples, it's a much tougher alternative for sunnier spots in the landscape.

DESIGN TIP

Before you rush out to the nursery, please remember to always check with your local cooperative extension office to find out if a plant is considered invasive in your area. Invasiveness is a regional issue, varying from state to state, so what may be considered a treasured plant in one area might very well be considered a noxious weed in yours.

VISUALLY LIGHT PLANTS

Helichrysum italicum
(curry plant)
- USDA Zones 7–10
- Full sun, low water

Miscanthus sinensis
'Morning Light' (maiden grass)
- USDA Zones 5–9
- Partial sun to sun, moderate water

Cotinus coggygria
'Ancot' (Golden Spirit smoke tree)
- USDA Zones 4–10
- Partial sun to sun, moderate to low water

This deer-resistant, drought-tolerant 2' × 2' (0.6m × 0.6m) perennial has deliciously scented foliage reminiscent of curry (though best to inhale and not ingest). In the summer, its pale yellow papery flowers on long white stalks seem to float above the tightly packed, narrow gray foliage below, simultaneously providing substance and lightness to the garden bed. The light colors are especially helpful in breaking up a primarily green garden, adding much-needed color contrast.

One of my favorite go-to grasses to break up a garden's oppressive atmosphere, the 'Morning Light's substantial size (5' × 2' [1.5m × 0.6m]) has a surprisingly airy appearance. Its thin green blades have creamy white margins that virtually glow when backlit by the sun (hence its name). A much less invasive variety (especially in cold and dry climates), this ornamental grass is the star of many of my gardens.

Smaller than its burgundy cousin (*Cotinus coggygria* 'Royal Purple'), this 8' × 6' (2.4m × 1.8m) deciduous shrub adds a bright, yet delicate, spotlight to the back of the border. Spectacular chartreuse foliage arrives in spring, matures to a brilliant gold in the summer and then changes again to coral, orange and red tones in the fall. Even its white and light pink summer blooms add an element of lightness to this shrub. It's the perfect antidote to a garden overflowing with dense, heavy and dark green shrubs.

COLOR

UNUSUAL SOURCES OF COLOR

Creating complex color echoes is one of the most rewarding (and addicting!) ways to weave a thread of harmony throughout your garden. In addition to the subtle colors contained within foliage, unusual color sources pulled from a plant's different elements are also instrumental in forming the basis for show-stopping seasonal highlights.

Sorbaria sorbifolia
'Sem' (false spirea)
• USDA Zones 2-8
• Partial sun to sun, moderate to low water

Nandina domestica 'Monum'
Plum Passion (heavenly bamboo)
• USDA Zones 4-10
• Partial sun to sun, low water

Phormium
'Sea Jade' (flax)
• USDA Zone 8-11
• Partial sun to sun, low water

Spring's new growth offers soft shades of salmon, yellow and chartreuse and provides the perfect opportunities to create unusual color combinations (imagine a *Heuchera* 'Peach Flambé' or a peachy million bells planted nearby). The summer foliage matures into a crisp green color, perfectly timed to highlight its emerging fluffy white flowers. A much-improved cultivar than older *Sorbaria* varieties, 'Sem' grows to a compact 4' × 4' (1.2m × 1.2m) size, is a less aggressive spreader and is very full and lush with graceful foliage.

This newer variety of heavenly bamboo has the deepest plum-colored new growth I've seen yet, arriving early spring and lasting through summer. It provides a dark and moody color echo when planted near burgundy-colored Japanese maples, Heucheras or coleus (providing visual weight and movement, as well). Taller than it is wide, it grows to 5' × 3' (1.5m × 0.9m), making it perfect for smaller spaces. Winter's cold temperatures give it a flush of bright red, complementing its clusters of rock-hard, red berries (perfect for holiday decorating).

Most varieties of *Phormium* leaves contain subtle color variations, making them ideal candidates for unusual color combinations. 'Sea Jade', with its olive green and burgundy mid stripe, is no exception. When paired with the yellow flowers of an Australian hibiscus (*Alyogyne hakeifolia* 'Yellow'), it is a study in subtle elegance. Growing just 4' × 2' (1.2m × 0.6m) with very upright foliage, it is suitable for smaller spaces and containers.

Heuchera
'Caramel' (coral bells and alum root)
- USDA Zones 4-9
- Partial sun to sun, moderate water

Coprosma repens
'Pink Splendor' (mirror plant)
- USDA Zones 8-11
- Partial sun to sun, low water

Solenostemon scutellarioides
'Honey Crisp' (coleus)
- USDA Zones—All
- Partial sun to sun, moderate water

Many gardeners consider heuchera a mainstay in the front of their borders, though it often comes as a surprise when they realize there's an entirely different color under the leaves. If the heuchera also has ruffled leaves, this hidden color will often flip up to reveal itself and, therefore, is an ideal opportunity to create a surprising color echo. 'Caramel' is a personal favorite as it has *H. villosa* in its parentage (meaning it's much more tolerant of sun, heat and humidity). Butterscotch-colored foliage emerges in the spring, with bright magenta colors hiding under each leaf.

The always-shiny foliage of the coprosma shrub often contains a rainbow of colors within each leaf, making it an ideal candidate for creating interesting color echoes. 'Pink Splendor' is a favorite among designers as the colors change throughout the year depending on the temperatures outside, ranging from pink (in the cold), to olive green (in the shade), to orange (in the heat). The ever-changing show of colors allows for unusual color combinations to be created from this versatile and low-maintenance shrub.

The many varieties of coleus are guaranteed to pack a colorful punch until fall's first killing frost. Whether trailing over a hanging basket or growing into a tidy 2' (0.6m) leafy mound or an eye-catching 4' (1.2m) focal point, they're not only fast growing, but they come in a seemingly endless array of colors (rich solid shades, subtle color variations and screaming splashes of colors). Similar to heuchera, the underside of the leaf oftentimes sports an entirely different color, providing one more opportunity to create a surprise color echo with nearby plantings.

Hydrangea macrophylla
'Lady in Red' (hydrangea)
• USDA Zones 6–9
• Partial sun, moderate water

Euphorbia griffithii
'Fireglow' (Griffith's spurge)
• USDA Zones 4–9
• Partial sun to sun, low water

Cestrum fasciculatum
'Newellii' (red cestrum)
• USDA Zones 8–11
• Partial sun to sun, moderate water

Flowers and colorful foliage tend to steal the show in gardens, but the other elements of a plant can also be used to help emphasize a particular color echo. 'Lady in Red' is a prime example, with cranberry-colored veins and stems working together to create a subtle color echo lasting several months in the garden. Its other attributes are it's mildew resistance, lacy pink flowers and compact 4' × 4' (1.2m × 1.2m) size, yet it's the subtle red coloration that I tend to value most.

While the vivid orange flowers (which are actually called bracts) are show-stopping, their colorful orange-red stems are even richer. In fact, it's the red tones in the stems that provide such a wonderful color echo alternative, pairing beautifully with a nearby dwarf purple fountain grass (Pennisetum setaceum 'Red Riding Hood') or a Nandina 'Firepower'. An excellent plant for dry, well-draining areas in your garden, it seems to thrive on neglect. All parts of the plant contain a milky sap that can be an irritant to some and is especially painful if ingested.

While the foliage and stems might be an ordinary shade of green, for many months out of the year this fast-growing shrub is also covered with a combination of delicate, dark pink, tubular flowers and cranberry-like clusters. The berries are dry and provide another opportunity for late summer color echoes in the garden. A hummingbird magnet, this towering 8' 6' (2.4m 1.8m) shrub is best placed at the back of the border to allow the weight of its claret-colored berries to gently drape over smaller perennials and annuals underneath. Imagine it paired with a 'Honeycrisp' coleus!

Malus hybrid
'Adams' (crabapple)
- USDA Zones 4–9
- Full sun, moderate water

Flower sprouts
'Petit Posy'
- USDA—All
- Full sun, moderate water

Rumex sanguineus
(bloody sorrel)
- USDA Zones 6–10
- Partial sun to full, moderate water

The beautiful 'Adams' crabapple grows new spring foliage in unusual shades of burgundy, maturing to green in the summer and to orange in the fall. But the show doesn't stop with the foliage, thanks to the late fall's show of cherry-red fruit (a valuable source of food for hungry birds, too). Consider planting the fall-blooming pineapple sage 'Golden Delicious' nearby to take advantage of the red flower/red berry knockout color echo. Moderately growing to 20' × 15' (6.1m × 4.6m), this is a very disease-resistant variety with some reports of hardiness down to Zone 3.

Don't forget to include colorful edibles in your ornamental garden bed as another unique source of color echoes. 'Petit Posy' sprout is a recent introduction (a cross between brussels sprouts and kale), sporting beautiful bi-colored, frilly, dusky plum-green foliage. It has fluffy edible "buttons" on the stem (delicious when sautéed like kale) and may be grown in full sun most any time of the year, withstanding all but the harshest of winters. Imagine it paired with 'Rozanne' geranium or the pale blooms of lavender (also edible!).

This tidy and colorful 15" × 15" (0.4m × 0.4m) perennial begs for a companion planting of red, pink or maroon to highlight its blood-red veins. Though the new leaves may be eaten like spinach, it may be an irritant to some, so I use them only as a garnish, placing a few leaves under wedges of cheese or piles of strawberries. To keep it returning reliably each spring, divide it every few years and remove tired-looking foliage during the heat of summer. In fact, should it start to look too tired, a simple buzz-cut to the ground will encourage new growth to sprout within two weeks.

TEXTURE

TOP TEXTURAL FLOWERS AND FOLIAGE

The adjectives used to describe texture in the garden are seemingly endless, ranging from *downy* and *soft* to *prickly* and *rough* and everything in between. However delightful textural plants might be to touch, it's important to remember they're powerful problem-solvers, as well.

Ptilotus exaltatus
'Joey' (pink mulla mulla)
• USDA Zones—All (Annual)
• Partial sun to full, low water

Persicaria polymorpha
(Giant Fleece Flower)
• USDA Zones 5–9
• Partial sun to sun, moderate water

Eryngium planum
'Blue Glitter' (sea holly)
• USDA Zones 5–9
• Full sun, low water

Considered an annual in all but the warmest climates, 'Joey' is welcome in my garden anytime. Thriving on neglect (one can easily love it to death with too much food and water), 'Joey' will reward you with months and months of prolific 3" to 4" (8cm to 10cm) bottlebrush blooms that glisten in shades of silver and neon pink. A natural magnet for butterflies and curious children alike, the feathery texture is almost too much to resist.

Another well-behaved persicaria, this vase-shaped, fast-growing herbaceous perennial tops out at 5' × 5' (1.5m × 1.5m) with a summer haze of white foamy flowers that float above the garden bed like a fluffy white cloud. Placed at the back of the border, it would be stunning with lower-growing contrasting textures, such as the serrated foliage of a dwarf oakleaf hydrangea ('Sikes Dwarf') or the smooth chartreuse foliage of Winter Glow Bergenia (*Bergenia cordifolia* 'Winterglut'). As if that weren't enough, it's tolerant of heat and humidity, as well.

A mid-sized textural delight to add to the garden, growing to a manageable 2½' × 1½' (0.8m × 0.5m), this perennial blooms from June through September with profuse egg-shaped, steel-blue colored flowers. Often confused with the common thistle, it also has deeply lobed and spiny leaves, but it isn't nearly as invasive. It adds beautiful (though sometimes painful) texture and unique color to the summer and fall garden and, once brought indoors, lasts a long time as a cut flower.

Salvia argentea
(silver sage)
- USDA Zones 5-10
- Full sun, low water

Melianthus major
'Antonow's Blue' (honey bush)
- USDA Zones 7-11
- Partial sun to sun, moderate to low water

Tanacetum ptarmiciflorum
(Silver Lace Bush)
- USDA Zones 8-10
- Full sun

Nothing begs to be touched more than the massive, downy foliage of the silver sage and, as such, it should be placed at the front of the border to tempt everyone who passes by. A short-lived perennial growing to 3' × 2' (0.9m × 0.6m), it has summer blooms of creamy white on slender stalks that add an additional 12" (0.3m) to its overall height. Silver sage may reseed or produce side shoots that can be removed (with roots) to propagate for the next generation.

Named for its faint scent of honey, the 1' to 2' (0.3m to 0.6m) long, distinctly toothed blue-gray-green leaves will cause the most jaded gardener to gasp in delight. Hardier and larger than the common species, 'Antonow's Blue' grows to an impressive 8' × 8' (2.4m × 2.4m) with enormous 12" (0.3m) reddish-brown, nectar-rich flowers that attract birds and butterflies alike. For smaller gardens, try the 'Purple Haze' selection, with hints of soft plum colors in its foliage growing to a manageable 3' × 3' (0.9m × 0.9m) size.

Though it looks delicate, this is one tough shrub! Growing to a compact 3' × 3' (0.9m × 0.9m) size, it's drought-tolerant and deer and rabbit resistant. Silver Lace Bush prefers sunny, dry sites with well-drained soil. It produces daisylike white flowers on stiff, upright branches late in the summer, but as they're somewhat unimpressive, I remove them to focus the plant's energy into producing more of the fantastic foliage. The bright and lacy foliage contrasts nicely with the smooth, darker foliage of a 'Blackbird' euphorbia or the purple blooms of the 'Munstead' lavender.

TEXTURE

TEXTURE WITH WEIGHT

In addition to a plant's color, its texture can also contribute much-needed weight (or lightness, for that matter) to the garden depending on how and when it's used. Different textures can offer different design solutions, such as anchoring a garden, adding lightness to a garden or even adding motion.

VISUALLY HEAVY TEXTURES

Rodgersia aesculifolia 'Bronze Peacock'

• USDA Zones 5–8

• Partial sun to sun, moderate water

Fatsia japonica 'Spider's Web' (Spider's Web Japanese aralia)

• USDA Zones 7–9

• Shade to partial sun, moderate water

Weigela florida 'Dark Horse' (weigela)

• USDA Zones 4–8

• Full sun, moderate water

This rodgersia's new growth arrives in spring in the shape of a peacock's tail in striking metallic shades of bronze and copper. Maturing to a shiny dark green, the thick, wrinkled and heavily veined foliage adds dramatic visual weight to a shady woodland garden. Growing to a compact 2' × 3' (0.6m × 0.9m) mound, this deer-resistant variety continues its dramatic show with complementary-colored pink flowers arriving in June through September. It's stunning surrounded by the fine foliage of a bleeding heart (*Dicentra spectabilis*) or Bowles' golden sedge (*Carex elata* 'Aurea').

Oversized, deeply lobed and leathery foliage tends to make quite a focal point in the garden, especially when each leaf is splashed with streaks of white. This rare tropical-looking shrub grows to a towering 8' × 8' (2.4m × 2.4m) and has complementing clusters of white flowers arriving in late fall. Though the oversized foliage provides visual weight to this shrub, the white variegation keeps it light enough to prevent it from overwhelming a smaller space.

A smaller version of the popular 'Wine and Roses' variety, the tidy 3' × 3' (0.9m × 0.9m) size makes 'Dark Horse' an ideal shrub for the middle of the border. I'm fond of the dark bronze, softly jagged foliage with its subtle lime-green venation—especially when backlit by the sun. Speaking of sun, the dark colors hold their own against the summer's sun, refusing to revert to the typical olive-green color common among plants with dark foliage.

VISUALLY LIGHT TEXTURES

Lavandula angustifolia
'Hidcote' (English lavender)
- USDA Zones 5–8
- Full sun, low water

Mahonia eurybracteata
'Soft Caress' (Oregon grape)
- USDA Zones 7–9
- Part sun to shade, moderate water

Melica altissima
'Atropurpurea' (Siberian melic grass)
- USDA Zones 4–8
- Partial sun to sun, moderate water

Named after England's Hidcote Manor, this variety is one of the most popular (and hardiest) dwarf lavenders on the market. Growing to a tidy 2' × 2' (0.6m × 0.6m) fragrant mound, the violet-purple blooms of 'Hidcote' retain their vibrant color well after the flowers are dried. While it's hardy to below 15°F (-9°C), fast-draining soil is a must as heavy, water-retaining soil means instant death as a result of root rot. The delicate needle-like foliage and tiny, nubby and densely packed flowers on top of the tall, slender wands give an airy quality to the front of the border.

A far cry from prickly and oversized mahonia of the past, the soft, slender foliage of this dwarf variety is a delight in the shady garden. Growing to a graceful (and manageable) 3' × 3' (0.9m × 0.9m) mound, the shiny and reflective, bamboo-like foliage adds an elegant and airy touch. Showy yellow flowers arrive in the late summer and last through early winter, providing a welcome burst of color, brightening up shady corners. Following the flowers are metallic blue berries that continue to add interest throughout the winter. It's truly a four-season plant.

Whether upright, fountain-shaped or drooping mounds, the graceful foliage of ornamental grass adds much needed motion with the slightest hint of a breeze. The Siberian melic grass, however, is a particularly stunning variety to add to the middle of the border. A clumping perennial growing to 4' × 4' (1.2m × 1.2m), the light green slender foliage has summer blooms (actually called inflorescence) on the ends of tall, stiff stalks that resemble one-sided, shaggy, chocolate-brown mustaches nodding in the wind.

TEXTURE

TOP EDIBLE TEXTURES

No longer banished to the back of the garden in out-of-the-way vegetable beds, edibles integrated throughout the entire garden is a trend that's caught on with gardeners everywhere. Why not take it a step further and include edibles that are both attractive enough to double as ornamentals and texturally interesting as well? Taste good, look good and feel good? What's not to love about these edibles?

Borago officinalis
(borage, starflower)

• USDA Zones—All

• Partial sun to sun, moderate water

This annual herb is a textural and visual delight that I often plant throughout my ornamental garden beds. The hairy (and somewhat prickly) leaves all but glow when backlit by the morning sun. Children love picking the sky-blue, star-shaped flowers and popping them in their mouths, as the taste is a refreshing combination of cucumbers and walnuts. Even though it's an annual herb, I jokingly refer to it as a perennial since I can guarantee its return each year thanks to its prolific reseeding nature.

Foeniculum vulgare
(fennel, sweet anise)

• USDA Zones 4–9

• Full sun, moderate water

Reliably returning each year, this licorice-flavored herb grows quickly to a towering 6' × 4' (1.8m × 1.2m) with bright green, delicate, cloud-like foliage. Blooming in July and August with dainty, yellow umbel-shaped flowers, it is also a valuable host plant for the Anise Swallowtail and Black Swallowtail butterflies. It has a tendency to reseed, but it can be controlled by removing spent flowers. Try the 'Bronze' fennel for foliage with bronzy-cinnamon colors.

Brassica oleracea 'Lacinato'
(dinosaur kale or Tuscan kale)

• USDA Zones 7–10, or annual

• Full sun, low water

This hearty, heirloom variety of kale is not only delicious when sautéed with olive oil and garlic, but it adds a unique textural touch to your ornamental garden bed, too. The thick, puckered, dark blue-green leaves (reminiscent to some of a dinosaur's skin) grow to an impressive 2' (0.6m) long, with the overall plant growing to just 2' × 2' (0.6m × 0.6m). This biannual is a cold-hardy variety (getting sweeter with the first kiss of frost) and will add much-needed textural interest to your winter garden.

TEXTURE

UNUSUAL SOURCES OF TEXTURE

When planning your garden, don't forget the more unusual sources of texture that plants provide. Elements such as stems, berries, dried seedpods or a tree's bark all help add an extra textural dimension to your garden. It's this extra dimension of interest that helps give your garden year-round interest.

Lunaria annua
(money plant, silver dollar plant)
• USDA Zones 5–9
• Partial sun to sun, moderate water

Cephalanthus occidentalis Sugar Shack
(dwarf buttonbush, honey balls)
• USDA Zones 4–10
• Partial sun to sun, moist conditions

Acer griseum
(paperbark maple)
• USDA Zones 4–8
• Partial sun to sun, moderate water

A favorite among children, this 3' × 2' (0.9m × 0.6m) biannual blooms April through May with purple flowers (or white, with the 'Alba' variety). It's the seedpods, however, that make this plant such a treasure in the textural garden, as they resemble flattened, paper-thin silver dollars. Maturing into a silvery, translucent wafer-thin disk, the seedpods also add delightful motion with the slightest breeze. In cooler climates, this biannual will produce only foliage the first year, but be patient and the following year you will be rewarded with colorful flowers and silver dollars.

Native to North America, this deciduous shrub is a much more garden-friendly size than its native cousin, growing to a manageable 4' × 4' (1.2m × 1.2m) size. White, compact, spherical flowers are produced in the summer and provide a valuable food source for birds and butterflies alike. However, it's the textural, rosy, ball-like fruits that form in the fall that provide the garden with stunning late-season interest.

One of the finest textural trees you can add to your winter garden, the sought-after paperbark maple is guaranteed to get the neighbors talking. Slow growing to 25' × 25' (7.6m × 7.6m), the summer's dark green, three-lobed foliage transforms into a fall sunset, in brilliant shades of bright orange and red. However, it's during the cold months of winter when the tree really shines as it sheds its orange-cinnamon colored bark in long curlicues that tempt anyone who passes by to reach out and touch.

FORMS AND SHAPES WITH WINTER INTEREST

Whether talking about two-dimensional shapes or three-dimensional forms, one thing is clear: each is vital for creating breathtaking year-round harmony. However subtle the differences may be, each element is distinctly different and, once understood, can be used to serve various functions in the garden.

Acer palmatum
'Sango-kaku' (coral bark maple)
- USDA Zones 5–8
- Partial sun to sun, moderate water

Morus alba
'Pendula' (Weeping mulberry)
- USDA Zones 4–8
- Partial sun to sun, moderate water

Betula pendula
(European white birch)
- USDA Zones 4–9
- Partial sun to sun, moderate water

'Sango-kaku' is one of my favorite Japanese maples, giving a show-stopping performance every day of the year. Its spring foliage emerges in bright shades of apple green, maturing to shimmering shades of yellow and gold with the first hint of fall. Once fall's show is over, however, the wispy stems and branches take their turn on the stage, turning brilliant shades of red and coral (thanks to colder temperatures). A mid-sized, vase-shaped tree growing to 15' × 15' (4.6m × 4.6m), this makes a perfect addition to a smaller garden.

Resembling a tiki-style thatched umbrella on a tropical beach, the dormant shape of this specimen tree is a sight to behold in the winter garden. This dwarf variety, growing to only 6' to 10' (1.8m to 3m), forms a curtain of thick, glossy, deeply lobed leaves throughout most of the year. Female varieties of the tree produce somewhat messy berries (which birds adore), while the male variety 'Chaparral' produces none.

Rivaling the grace of any Japanese maple is the European birch, with its crisp, white slender trunk, upright main branches and graceful, weeping side branches that gently sway in the wind. Spring and summer find it covered with delicate and finely cut bright green leaves that mature to golden shades of yellow with the first cold temperatures. Continuing the interest through bleak winter months is the fresh-as-fallen-show white trunk and branches, so beautifully silhouetted against a cold, blue sky.

Cornus sanguinea 'Cato' Arctic Sun
(bloodtwig dogwood)
- USDA Zones 4–7
- Partial sun to sun, moderate water

Ilex meserveae
'Hachfee' Castle Spire (blue holly)
- USDA Zones 5–7
- Partial sun to sun, moderate water

Thuja occidentalis
'Techny Gold'
- USDA Zones 3–7
- Partial sun to sun, moderate water

Unlike its larger cousins, this dwarf variety grows to a manageable 3' × 4' (0.9m × 1.2m), making it an ideal shrub for the smaller garden. Its normally green leaves transform into shades of peachy-orange and golden yellow in the fall. The true show happens, however, in the winter months when the slender upright twigs turn golden shades of yellow tipped with red—a spectacular sight to behold when set against a snowy backdrop.

Whether used as a foundation plant, hedge or specimen shrub, the compact, pyramidal form of this holly grows to just 6' to 10' (1.8m to 3m) and is one of the best varieties for year-round interest. Dark green, glossy, pointed leaves are held tight through the year, with brilliant red berries in the fall and winter (a valuable food source for hungry birds). Considered one of the bones of the garden, its dense form allows it to stand up to mounds of winter snow, giving the garden shape and definition when it needs it most.

This colorful, tough evergreen shrub has some of the showiest foliage I've seen. Whereas many other gold varieties tend to lose their color during cold, winter months, 'Techny Gold' remains vibrant, adding a much-needed splash of color to the winter landscape. The finely cut needles are densely packed, giving this shrub its conical form, reaching heights of 10' to 15' (3m to 4.6m) in the garden. Used as a foundation plant, hedge or specimen, this shrub is valuable in providing year-round structure in the garden.

FORM AND SHAPE

FORMS AND SHAPES WITH VISUAL MOVEMENT

Though static in nature, many forms and shapes of plants provide the illusion of movement in the garden. Whether directing the line of sight up, down or swirling around like a pinwheel, their unusual forms are one more way to create a dynamic and unique garden experience.

Lotus maculatus
'Gold Flash' (parrot's beak)
- USDA Zones 9–11
- Partial sun to sun, moderate water

Euphorbia myrsinites
(donkeytail spurge)
- USDA Zones 5–9
- Partial sun to full sun, low water

Aloe polyphylla
(spiral aloe)
- USDA Zones 7–9
- Partial sun to sun, low water

The colorful orange and red flowers look like the flames of a fire, drawing the eye upward. Tolerant of heat and humidity, this tender perennial will reward you with months of "flames" starting in mid-spring and continuing through the fall. Once it stops blooming, just shake off the spent flowers, feed it with your favorite organic fertilizer and sit back to watch another colorful show. Growing to just 9" × 3' (0.2m × 0.9m) it's best used as a ground cover or trailing from a container or hanging basket. Hummingbirds, bees and butterflies love this beautiful garden treat.

This tough-as-nails perennial appears to spiral along in tight, concentric geometric patterns, whether gently draping over stone walls, down the sides of containers or sprawling along the ground. This low-growing euphorbia will slowly form a 3' (0.9m) mat while only reaching 12" (0.3m) high. Late winter through spring finds the ends of the long blue-green spirals topped with airy sprays of acid-yellow flowers, lasting for weeks at a time. All parts of the plant contain a milky sap that is toxic to varying degrees, so use protection when handling. It's resistant to drought, heat and deer.

Stare at this succulent for long and you might start to feel dizzy thanks to its spiraling clockwise (or counterclockwise) growth pattern. Forming a stemless, solitary rosette that grows 1' × 2' (0.3m × 0.6m), this variety is a fascinating specimen for a container or succulent garden. Each plant has five rows of leaves growing in concentric patterns, with each leaf tapering to a point with jagged "teeth" along the edges. Occasionally, it blooms with clusters of salmon-pink flowers that dangle from a long and slender stem. It's a textural delight with jaw-dropping form for any mild-climate garden.

Viburnum plicatum
'Summer Snowflake'
- USDA Zones 5–9
- Partial sun to full sun, moderate water

Phormium tenax
'Maori Maiden' (flax)
- USDA Zones 8–11
- Partial sun, low water

Cupressus cashmeriana
(Kashmir cypress)
- USDA Zones 7–9
- Partial sun to full sun, moderate water

The tiered, horizontal branches of this deciduous shrub magnificently display huge clusters of snowy white flowers that draw the eye sideways in either direction. In this larger variety, growing to 8' × 10' (2.4m × 3m), the flat-topped flowers cover the entire length of the branches, appearing in late spring and lasting through summer. The dark green, deeply furrowed foliage turns shades of reddish-maroon in the fall, followed by ornamental red berries that hungry birds devour. It's a stunning shrub for the back of the border.

Like vertical explosions in all directions, the long, strappy foliage of 'Maori Maiden' will add visual excitement to the sleepiest of gardens. The smooth, polished leaves in warm shades of apricot, pink and olive-green harmonize beautifully with neighboring plants with yellow, purple or burgundy flowers. Its manageable 3' × 3' (0.9m × 0.9m) size makes it ideal for the middle of the border or growing in a container. To avoid sunburn, plant this particular variety in partial sun. Hummingbirds adore the annual show of its otherworldly spires of garnet red flowers that last for weeks.

Like a cascading blue-green waterfall, the finely cut needles of the Kashmir cypress drape to the ground on long, pendulous branches, casting feathery shadows below. A rare specimen that would add untold grace and beauty to warm-climate gardens, this remarkable, yet fragile, treasure is worth the hunt and hassle to site it just right (no damaging cold, wind or heat, please!). It grows to a towering 40' × 20' (12m × 6m) with a graceful, narrow pyramidal form.

FORM AND SHAPE

FORMS AND SHAPES WITH VISUAL WEIGHT

To create a well-balanced garden, all of its different layers need to harmonize with one another. Contrast and repetition are important not only in terms of a plant's color and texture but its form and shape as well. One component of a well-balanced garden is the visual weight created by various plants that helps prevent a space from appearing overly oppressive, overly chaotic or lopsided in appearance.

VISUALLY HEAVY PLANTS

Canna
'Intrigue'
- USDA Zones 7–11
- Partial sun to sun, moderate water

Picea pungens
'Glauca Compacta' (blue spruce)
- USDA Zones 3–8
- Partial sun to sun, moderate water

Cercidiphyllum japonicum
'Pendulum' (weeping katsura tree)
- USDA Zones 4–8
- Full sun, moderate water

The *Canna's* dramatic and oversized foliage, with its smooth and silky texture and paddle-like shape, are destined to become focal points, making quite a statement in the perennial garden. Varieties, such as 'Intrigue', with dark green and maroon colors, are vital in adding significant visual weight to a garden bed, helping to anchor neighboring light and airy plants. Blooming summer through fall, cannas add a tropical touch to the garden, quickly growing to 6' to 10' (1.8m to 3m) in the garden or 3' to 5' (0.9m to 1.5m) in containers.

The dense pyramidal shape of this showy evergreen shrub, with its small, tightly packed blue needles, adds significant visual weight to the garden. Slow-growing to 12' × 15' (3.7m × 4.6m), 'Glauca Compacta' is best used as a specimen plant or as one of the garden's bones. The crisp and sharp texture not only packs a visual punch to the garden bed, but its evergreen form steadfastly carries the garden through the year. 'Montgomery' dwarf is a smaller variety, growing to 4' × 3' (1.2m × 0.9m), with a compact pyramidal shape.

The gentle, weeping form of this deciduous tree creates an eye-catching specimen in any garden. Slow-growing to 15' to 20' (4.6m to 6.1m) wide and 10' to 15' (3m to 4.6m) tall, the tree's stiff, thin branches fan out from the crown and gracefully drape to the ground like a shimmering curtain. Sugary scented, heart-shaped foliage emerges in spring with bronze-red tones; it matures to blue-green in the summer and ends with a golden yellow show in the fall.

VISUALLY LIGHT PLANTS

Polygonatum odoratum
(Solomon's seal)
• USDA Zones 3–9
• Shade to partial sun, moist conditions

Muhlenbergia capillaris
Regal Mist (pink muhly)
• USDA Zones 6–9
• Partial sun to sun, moderate water

Rhamnus alaternus
'Variegata' (variegated buckthorn)
• USDA Zones 7–9
• Partial sun to sun, low water

While the teardrop-like flowers are certainly delightful, as are the black seedpods that follow, the graceful arching stems and lance-shaped foliage are what give this perennial such charm in the woodland garden. Depending on the variety, Solomon's seal grows anywhere from 1' to 4' (0.3m to 1.2m) high and slowly spreads via shallow rhizomes to form 3' (0.9m) colonies (even in areas notoriously difficult due to crowded tree roots). The end of the season is signaled by a show of golden yellow.

Like a mist of pink haze gently floating over your garden, pink muhly is one of the lightest grasses of all. Quickly growing to 4' × 4' (1.2m × 1.2m) and needing nothing more than a weekly watering and a late-winter prune, this low-maintenance grass is invaluable for providing shimmering lightness and a soft pink glow to the fall garden.

Though large in stature (quickly growing to 15' × 15' [4.6m × 4.6m]), the delicate-looking gray-green leaves with creamy white margins help to create a feeling of lightness and have a luminous appearance when placed against a dark background. This tough and fast-growing shrub makes an ideal hedge or screen in smaller gardens, where lightness is vital to maintain an open atmosphere. Two added bonuses are its spring show of white flowers (echoing the foliage color) and vibrant red berries in the fall and winter.

FORM AND SHAPE

FORMS AND SHAPES IN THE GARDEN

More than a just a novelty, plants with unique forms add endless opportunities for contrast and repetition, practical problem solving and optical illusions. With a basic understanding of how a plant's form and shape can be used functionally in the garden, you can begin to transform your garden from the bones on up.

EXCLAMATION POINTS

Reseda luteola
(dyer's rocket)
- USDA Zones 5–9
- Partial sun to sun, moderate water

Berberis thunbergii
'Orange Rocket' (barberry)
- USDA Zones 4–9
- Full sun, low water

Ginkgo biloba
'Princeton Sentry' (Maidenhair Tree)
- USDA Zones 3–9
- Full sun, moderate water

The long, slender spires of small yellow flowers appear to reach for the heavens as they rocket skyward, then demurely nod downward. An old-world plant valued for its sweet fragrance, dyer's rocket begins blooming mid-spring and lasts through summer, adding a 3' × 3' (0.9m × 0.9m) soft yellow cloud to the garden. It is best started from seed as it resents transplanting. Use caution when handling, as it may irritate the skin.

The tight, missile-shaped habit of this colorful barberry slowly grows to 6' × 2' (1.8m × 0.6m), making it an ideal candidate for tight, sunny spaces. The vibrant coral-orange new foliage ages to green, then again to ruby red in the fall, providing endless opportunities to create color echoes. Just imagine it planted near a blanket flower (*Gaillardia* 'Arizona Sun') or tickseed (*Coreopsis* 'Pineapple Pie'). Whereas other varieties may be invasive and disease-prone, 'Orange Rocket' has improved resistance to rust with non-viable seeds.

There's something magical about a ginkgo tree in the fall, with its show of brilliant gold foliage shimmering with the slightest breeze. 'Princeton Sentry' grows to a towering 40' × 15' (12.2 m × 4.6m), fitting snugly into narrow spaces where other trees would not. The delicate fan-shaped foliage emerges in the spring in bright green colors that are stunning when backlit by the morning sun. The highly anticipated fall show lasts for several weeks, until the foliage drops all at once, leaving a spectacular golden carpet below.

GLOBES AND SPHERES

Gomphrena haageana
'Strawberry Fields' (globe amaranth)
- USDA Zones—All, Annual
- Full sun, moderate water

Available in a wide range of colors, the variety 'Strawberry Fields' has the truest red flowers (called *bracts*) with a papery texture that resembles tiny strawberries lightly bobbing on long, slender stems. Profuse flowering begins in summer and lasts through the first frost, providing excellent cut flowers to either bring indoors or to use for drying. Mostly grown as an annual, the 2' × 2' (0.6m × 0.6m) globe amaranth may sometimes overwinter in milder climates.

Picea pungens 'Glauca Globosa'
(dwarf globe blue spruce)
- USDA Zones 2–8
- Partial sun to sun, moderate water

This slow-growing 4' × 4' (1.2m × 1.2m) evergreen shrub has a naturally rounded shape with bright blue foliage. The short, stiff needles hold their color throughout the year but are brightest as they first emerge in spring. This easy-care shrub makes an attractive anchor in the perennial garden bed, helping to add year-round interest as well as visual weight. Due to its unique color and form, the 'Glauca Globosa' is best appreciated with complementary plants nearby, such as the soft blue Ground Morning Glory (*Convolvulus mauritanicus*) or soft yellow million bells (*Calibrachoa*).

Olea europaea
Little Ollie (dwarf olive shrub)
- USDA Zones 8–10
- Full sun, moderate water

This non-fruiting olive tree behaves more like a shrub as it naturally (and slowly) grows into a 6' × 6' (1.8m × 1.8m) compact, round shape, adding evergreen year-round interest (and a taste of the Mediterranean) to warm-climate gardens. The narrow, deep green leaves have silver-gray undersides and are very disease-resistant as well as drought-, heat- and salt-tolerant. It's stunning when paired with the bright blue flowers of a plumbago (*Ceratostigma plumbaginoides*) or the soft purple spires of lavender (*Lavandula* spp.)

FOUNTAINS AND VASES

Crocosmia
'Walbreyes' (Bright Eyes montbretia)
- USDA Zones 6–10
- Full sun, moderate water

Yucca filamentosa
'Color Guard' (variegated yucca)
- USDA Zones 4–10
- Full sun, low water

Hamamelis × intermedia
'Pallida' (witch hazel)
- USDA Zones 5–8
- Partial sun to sun, moderate water

A favorite among hummingbirds and gardeners alike, the upright-facing vivid yellow and orange blooms of 'Walbreyes' are guaranteed to add a much-needed shot of color to the tired, late summer garden bed. A dwarf variety, the 2' × 2' (0.6m × 0.6m) fountain-shaped 'Walbreyes' is an ideal candidate for the front of the border. While the flowers might look delicate, this perennial thrives in hot conditions. Divide the clumps every two or three years to keep the plant blooming.

The dramatic and colorful sword-like leaves of this 2' × 5' (0.6m × 1.5m) upright yucca are a bold addition to the middle of the border. Impressive ivory spires of fragrant cup-shaped blooms add an additional 4' (1.2m) to the foliage mid-summer and are a favorite among ladybugs and hummingbirds. Whether used to anchor a free-flowing perennial garden bed or as an accent plant in a container, this plant is a must-have for any gardener wishing to add year-round contrasting texture and form. It's evergreen in all but the coldest climates and also deer-, drought- and heat-resistant.

The cheery yellow, sugary-scented fringe-like flowers of witch hazel dangle from the large, vase-shaped shrub. Quickly growing to a towering 10' × 10' (3m × 3m), 'Pallida' can easily crowd many gardens if not kept under control with judicious pruning. Cutting a fourth of the canes to the ground each year in spring (after flowering) will help regenerate healthy new growth while keeping these somewhat overly rambunctious shrubs under control. For smaller spaces, consider the 'Angelly' variety with distinctly upright growth to 3' (0.9m).

Edgeworthia chrysantha
(paper bush plant)
- USDA Zones 7–9
- Full shade to part sun, moderate water

Chamelaucium 'Matilda'
(waxflower)
- USDA Zones 9–11
- Full sun, moderate water

Cotinus coggygria
'Royal Purple' (smoke tree)
- USDA Zones 4–9
- Partial sun to sun, low water

A treasure in the late-winter garden, the intoxicating perfume from the creamy yellow flower clusters fills the air with Daphne-like fragrance for months at a time. A moderate grower to 8' × 8' (2.4m × 2.4m), the deciduous shrub begins leafing out in spring with slender, blue-green foliage that turns golden yellow with fall's first cold temperatures. When branches are bare, the multi-stemmed mounding shape and light, cinnamon-colored stems add tremendous architectural value and an elegant silhouette to the bare winter garden.

Unlike its towering cousins, Matilda is a mild-mannered compact grower, slowly forming a 3' x 3' (0.9m x 0.9m) mound. Its light-green, narrow, needle-like foliage looks good year-round, but this shrub really shines in late winter. Deliciously fragrant small white flowers emerge in November, slowly developing a reddish-pink tinge on the petals, maturing to a solid dark pink color (oftentimes mixing on the plant at the same time) and lasting well into March. If you're lucky, you might be rewarded with a surprise performance of repeat blooms throughout the rest of the year.

To see a smoke tree in full bloom is nothing short of magical, but this large mounding shrub has so much more to offer in addition to the early summer's frothy haze. The dark purple-red foliage carries this deciduous shrub through spring and summer, making it a valuable "bone" of the garden bed. When fall arrives, the foliage continues the show by turning brilliant shades of crimson. Quickly growing to 15' × 15' (4.6m × 4.6m), it can be kept smaller by pruning mid-summer (after it blooms). For a knockout combination, plant this maroon beauty near chartreuse foliage.

CONES

Vitex agnus-castus var. *latifolia*
(chastetree)
- USDA Zones 6–9
- Full sun, low water

Pittosporum tenuifolium
'Tasman Ruffles' (pittosporum)
- USDA Zones 7–10
- Partial sun to sun, moderate water

Pinus flexilis
'Vanderwolf's Pyramid' (limber pine)
- USDA Zones 2–7
- Full sun, moderate water

A fantastic alternative for those in warmer climates unable to grow beloved lilacs, the chastetree produces magnificent 10" to 20" (0.25m to 0.5m) conical lilac-blue flowers from summer through fall. This fast-growing, deciduous, multi-trunked shrub quickly grows to 15' × 20' (4.6m × 6m), making it ideal to plant at the back of the border. The size of the shrub can be kept significantly smaller, however, with late winter pruning. Don't let its delicate and showy blooms fool you; Vitex is deer-, drought- and heat-resistant and thrives in difficult garden settings.

Evergreen, low-water and available in a range of sizes, the many varieties of *Pittosporum* are commonly associated with low-maintenance hedging plants. 'Tasman Ruffles', however, is distinctly different, with its dainty olive-green leaves with gently ruffled edges and its unique dense, pyramidal shape. Though delicate in appearance, 'Tasman Ruffles' is one of the hardiest selections of pittosporum. The thin black stems provide an excellent opportunity to create a unique color combination (imagine it planted near a *Sambucus* Black Lace, or an *Anthriscus sylvestris* 'Ravenswing').

With its twisted, silvery blue-green needles growing on graceful, dense branches, 'Vanderwolf's Pyramid' is a superior selection for a specimen tree. The limber pine, with its distinctive pyramidal form, grows to 25' × 15' (7.6m × 4.6m) and has multi-colored needles that shimmer when backlit by the morning sun. Despite its graceful appearance, this tree is tough as nails with the ability to adapt to dry and windy conditions as well as areas where soils are thin and poor. As if that weren't enough, the limber pine is also resistant to insects, disease and deer.

MATS

Geranium × cantabrigiense
'Biokovo' (cranesbill geranium)
• USDA Zones 4–9
• Partial sun, moderate water

Taxus cuspidata 'Monloo'
(Emerald Spreader Japanese yew)
• USDA Zones 4–7
• Partial sun to sun, moderate water

Cotoneaster dammeri 'Streib's Findling'
(Bearberry cotoneaster)
• USDA Zones 6–9
• Full sun, moderate water

One of my favorites for semi-shady areas, 'Biokovo' is a fast-growing, tough little perennial perfect for covering the bare legs of woody shrubs, growing between the crevices of a stone wall or visually grounding a perennial bed to its site. This fast-forming mat appears light and delicate, due to its small-lobed foliage and dainty pale pink flowers (with long seedpods that resemble a crane's bill) while quickly growing to smother out weeds. It spreads by underground stems with very shallow roots that are a snap to remove and transplant to other parts of the garden.

When looking for an exceptionally cold-hardy, low-maintenance ground cover that holds its color throughout the coldest winter months, the low-growing 'Monloo' might be just the answer. Spreading to over 10' (3m) wide and only 30" (0.8m) tall, the attractive dark green foliage will gracefully drape over retaining walls or walkway edges while standing up to foot and road traffic. The beautiful evergreen is also an attractive mat to plant at the base of more high-profile upright shrubs.

Many varieties of Cotoneaster can be described as both tough and hardy and graceful and colorful. 'Streib's Findling', is an excellent-spreading ground cover with a stunning herringbone silhouette. One of the lowest-growing Cotoneasters, reaching only 6" (0.2m) high by 8' (2.4m) wide, it's covered with dense, tiny, blue-green evergreen leaves dotted with tiny white flowers in the spring. Cherry-red berries that last for months follow the flowers. Drought and deer resistance makes this fast-growing mat ideal for tough gardening situations.

PHOTO CREDITS

All photos by Rebecca Sweet except as noted below.

A hearty 'thank-you!' to the following for allowing the author to use their images on these pages:

Page 28: Snowy arbor by Angela Davis

Page 124: *Primula vulgaris* 'Drumcliff' by Patrick Fitzgerald

Page 125: *Cotinus coggygria* 'Ancot' by Andrew Keys

Page 135: *Lunaria annua* by Melanie Dorausch Vassallo

Page 135: *Cephalanthus occidentalis* Sugar Shack by Proven Winners

Page 137: *Ilex meserveae* 'Hachfee' Castle Spire by Proven Winners

Page 137: *Thuja occidentalis* 'Techny Gold' by Proven Winners

Page 141: *Muhlenbergia capillaris* Regal Mist by Monrovia

Page 144: *Crocosmia* 'Walbreyes' by Monrovia

Page 146: *Pittosporum tenuifolium* 'Tasman Ruffles' by Monrovia

Page 147: *Taxus cuspidata* 'Monloo' by Monrovia

Page 147: *Cotoneaster dammeri* 'Streib's Findling' by Monrovia

Talented gardeners (professional or not!) whose breathtaking gardens are featured in this book:

Pages 2, 13, 74: Lani Freymiller

Pages 4, 5, 13, 92, 117: Linda Anderson

Pages 13, 63, 72–73, 75, 85, 91, 94, 98, 99, 101, 111, 112, 119: Freeland and Sabrina Tanner

Page 28: Angela Davis

Page 46: Lisa Mitchell

Page 80: Linda Allard

Many of my photos were taken at these public gardens:

Pages 25, 68, 120: Elizabeth Gamble Gardens, Palo Alto, California

Page 26, 42, 76, 78: Stonecrop Gardens, Cold Spring, New York

Page 40: Filoli, Woodside, California

Page 51: J. Paul Getty Museum, Los Angeles, California

Page 63, 109: Innisfree, Millbrook, New York

Pages 64, 77, 104: Cornerstone Gardens, Sonoma, California

Page 68: The Oregon Garden, Silverton, Oregon

Page 80: Annie's Annuals & Perennials, Richmond, California

Pages 86, 144: Washington Park Arboretum, Seattle, Washington

Page 103: Sunset Test Gardens, Menlo Park, California

RESOURCES

I'm a big believer in supporting local, independent nurseries whenever possible. When you are looking for a specific plant, a helpful nursery will do everything they can to find an alternative source so they can special order that plant for you. Sometimes, though, after all of their effort, they may still come up empty handed. If this happens to you, check with some of my favorite online nurseries:

MAIL ORDER SOURCES FOR PLANTS

Annie's Annuals & Perennials
www.anniesannuals.com

Bluestone Perennials
www.bluestoneperennials.com

Cistus Nursery
www.cistus.com

Digging Dog Nursery
www.diggingdog.com

Lazy S's Farm Nursery
www.lazyssfarm.com

Plant Delights Nursery
www.plantdelights.com

Canada
Bluestem Nursery
www.bluestem.ca

Bōtanus
www.botanus.com

HELPFUL WEBSITES

Arbor Day Foundation
www.arborday.org
Tree identification, hardiness zones, tree selection and planting

eXtension
www.extension.org
Objective, research-based gardening information throughout the nation

Floridata
www.floridata.com
Huge nation-wide plant encyclopedia

Lady Bird Johnson Wildflower Center
www.wildflower.org
Search for native plants by region.

National Gardening Association
www.garden.org/zipzone
USDA Zone map

Regional Master Gardener programs and websites
www.ahs.org/gardening-resources/master-gardeners
An invaluable source of relevant, local and useful information

UC Davis Arboretum All-Stars
www.arboretum.ucdavis.edu
Top 100 drought-tolerant plants for the west coast.

INDEX

Refresh Your Garden Design With Color, Texture & Form. Copyright © 2013 by Rebecca Sweet. Manufactured in China. All rights reserved. No part of this book may be reproduced in any form or by any electronic or mechanical means including information storage and retrieval systems without permission in writing from the publisher, except by a reviewer who may quote brief passages in a review. Published by Horticulture, an imprint of F+W Media, Inc., 10151 Carver Road, Suite 200, Blue Ash, Ohio, 45242. (800) 289-0963. First Edition.

Other fine Horticulture products are available from your favorite bookstore, garden store or online supplier. Visit our websites at www.hortmag.com and www.gardenershub.com.

17 16 15 14 13   5 4 3 2 1

ISBN 9781440330407

Distributed in Canada by Fraser Direct
100 Armstrong Avenue
Georgetown, ON, Canada L7G 5S4
Tel: (905) 877-4411

Distributed in the U.K. and Europe
by F&W Media International LTD
Brunel House, Forde Close, Newton Abbot, TQ12 4PU, UK
Tel: (+44) 1626 323200, Fax: (+44) 1626 323319
E-mail: enquiries@fwmedia.com

Distributed in Australia by Capricorn Link
P.O. Box 704, S. Windsor NSW, 2756 Australia
Tel: (02) 4260-1600, Fax (02) 4577-5288
E-mail: books@capricornlink.com.au

EDITED BY *Christine Doyle*

DESIGNED BY *Christy Cotterman*

PRODUCTION COORDINATED BY *Debbie Thomas*

INVASIVE PLANT DISCLAIMER

An invasive plant is generally considered one that is non-native and has an adverse effect on its surrounding natural habitat. These invasive plants can cause a significant amount of damage to the surrounding ecosystem by overwhelming native vegetation, harboring damaging pests or even altering the genetic makeup of native species.

Just because you can carefully contain your invasive plant's roots, don't forget that many plants propagate by seed (thanks to the wind, birds or other small animals). When these seeds escape into the surrounding ecosystem, serious damage can occur to the surrounding environment.

For the reasons mentioned above, a plant's inclusion in this book is not a guarantee that it's suitable for your area. Before buying any new plant, it's advisable to first check to see if it's considered an invasive in your region. Information on regional invasive plants can be found on the website for the Center for Invasive Species and Ecosystem Health, www.invasive.org.

METRIC CONVERSION CHART

To convert	to	multiply by
Inches	Centimeters	2.54
Centimeters	Inches	0.4
Feet	Centimeters	30.5
Centimeters	Feet	0.03
Yards	Meters	0.9
Meters	Yards	1.1

MEET REBECCA

Rebecca Sweet is a garden designer and owner of the design firm Harmony in the Garden, located in Northern California. Her gardens have been featured in *Sunset*, *Fine Gardening*, *Horticulture*, *Woman's Day* and *Country Living* magazines as well as many gardening books and regional newspapers and publications. Rebecca and her gardens have also been featured on the critically acclaimed PBS series *Growing a Greener World*, and she has been a radio guest on *GardenLife* and *Martha Stewart Living*.

In addition to designing gardens, Rebecca is co-author of the best-selling *Garden Up! Smart Vertical Gardening for Small and Large Spaces* (Cool Springs Press, 2011). Rebecca also shares her secrets to successful garden design in her column "Harmony in the Garden" in *Horticulture* magazine. In her popular blog "Gossip in the Garden," Rebecca shares gardening tips, design strategies and how-to videos for both the novice and experienced gardener.

It's easy to get to know Rebecca better— chat with her on Facebook or Twitter, or leave a comment on her blog.

Follow Rebecca on Twitter **@SweetRebecca**
Read Rebecca's blog at **www.gossipinthegarden.com**
View her design portfolio at **www.harmonyinthegarden.com**

FREE DOWNLOAD

GARDENING COLOR WHEEL
COLOR SOLUTIONS FOR YOUR GARDEN

These free worksheets teach you how to solve five common garden problems by using color. Plus you'll receive three beautiful garden color wheels that demonstrate various garden color schemes and concepts. These worksheets are perfect for use on site in your garden.

Visit **<www.hortmag.com/gardencolorwheel>** for your free downloads.

Get more gardening advice and sign up for our free e-newsletter at **<www.hortmag.com>**

Like us for special offers and giveaways: **<facebook.com/HorticultureMagazine>**